LETTERS FROM THE ORANGE EMPIRE

Washington navel oranges showing blue-mold decay.
Frontispiece of U.S.D.A. Bureau of Plant Industry Bulletin 123 (1908)

Letters from the Orange Empire

By G. HAROLD POWELL

Edited by
RICHARD G. LILLARD

Afterword by
LAWRENCE CLARK POWELL

LOS ANGELES

HISTORICAL SOCIETY OF SOUTHERN CALIFORNIA

1990

In Memoriam
Richard Gordon Lillard
June 3, 1909–March 19, 1990

CONTENTS

Introduction

THE "POWELL ERA" IN THE
CALIFORNIA CITRUS INDUSTRY

I

THE YEAR WAS 1908, the occasion, a California Fruit Growers' Convention, the speaker, John Henry Reed, his subject, "The Proper Handling of Citrus Fruits." Reed, a leading orange grower, praised G. Harold Powell, the U.S. Department of Agriculture pomologist whose investigations had given "new money values" to orange crops. Reed exclaimed over the speed with which growers had adopted Powell recommendations that saved growers from losses of more than a million dollars a year. Reed said, "This may . . . be known as the Powell era in the history of the California orange industry."[1]

Other speakers at the conference eulogized Powell. A lemon grower thanked him for lessons on how and when to pick lemons and to pack and ship them. Professor E. J. Wickson of the University of California Agriculture Department said, "The demand for research in agricultural lines is broader and sharper than it ever was before in California, and it is producing the most gratifying results, such, for instance, as the result of the studies of Mr. Powell and his associates."[2]

A month before, on March 31, the United States Department of Agriculture had issued "The Decay of Oranges While in Transit from California," Bulletin 123 of the Bureau of Plant Industry. The work of Powell and five assistants, it reported on an unprecedented investigation over a period of four years, involving the actual handling and careful inspection of large quantities of fruit on a commercial scale the entire way from Southern California orchards to auctions and markets in the East. It had involved, too, the use of laboratory

1

methods to the fullest extent practicable. Colored plates in Bulletin 123 showed the fungoid causes of loss in transit, sooty-mold on Valencia oranges and blue-mold on Washington navels.

Bulletin 123 stood as one of the first investigations "in which the results of a study could be correlated clearly with demonstrated financial savings that outweighed the cost of research many times over."[3]

And even earlier in the year, at nearby Pachappa, the grower Cornelius Earle Rumsey had placed a plaque on his new packing house: "In gratitude to the U.S. Dep't. of Agriculture, the Bureau of Plant Industry, G. Harold Powell, Pomologist, and His Staff, This Building is Dedicated to the Careful Handling of Citrus Fruit. January 10th, 1908."[4]

II

These accolades, and there were a great many others in the daily and agricultural press, stimulated the self-confidence and the ambitions of a many-sided person, a family man, a laboratory and field scientist, a highly skilled manager of people, a humanist with appreciation of the arts, and a captivating dinner-table conversationalist and public speaker. He quickly became an agricultural leader, and he remains permanently a representative figure for his "era."

He exemplifies the rise of the research biologist and a major shift in the farmer's economy from independence, often shaky, to membership in a producer's cooperative with security and stability, and progress from traditional farming methods such as planting orchards with seeds to planting selected, improved varieties grafted on appropriate rootstocks. Johnny Appleseed and rule of thumb were giving way to the evident results of studies done by land-grant colleges and by State and Federal bureaus and departments. Government and agriculture joined to control disease and raise more food.

In his own short life (1872–1922) Powell evolved from nineteenth century youth to twentieth century urban maturity, from provincial Northeastern perspectives during peaceful decades to national and international concerns during the Great War. He played an active part in the growth of agricultural economics as a field of everyday practical concern. He helped lead a boom in land and labor productivity.

He joined the migration of educated, talented, successful Easterners to Southern California in the golden age of family horticulture on
the rich, irrigated soils of the citrus empire that by 1900 stretched
eastward from Santa Barbara County through portions of Ventura,
Los Angeles, Orange, and San Bernardino counties to Riverside
County with its queen City of Riverside, a place to winter much
enjoyed by Canadians and East-coast Americans with money.

Powell figures in the early decades of the twentieth century, when
the American diet was expanding from such traditional foods as
potatoes, wheat, and apples to include "luxuries" — Mediterranean or
"subtropical" delights such as oranges, grapefruit, tangerines, and
avocados ("alligator pears"). In 1907 the California Fruit Growers'
Exchange began to advertise, starting in Iowa with "Orange Week."
In time the Exchange would lead the public to see citrus fruit as an
essential of daily diet and make Sunkist the best known brand of fresh
fruit in the world. In Southern California, as elsewhere, farmers
began to specialize, citrus in Florida, apples in Washington State,
strawberries in North Carolina, or peaches in Michigan and Georgia.
As regional self-sufficiency declined, the problem arose of how to
transport fresh, perishable crops by railroad over long distances to
market. The government's man, Powell, was among those at hand,
trained to solve such problems.

III

The lives of some women and men, certainly Powell's life, are all of a
piece. His family was Quaker and prosperously rural. His grandfather and father grew apples on Hudson Valley farms near Ghent.
His father, who lectured and wrote on pomology and floriculture,
founded the New York State Agricultural Service, and took charge of
the New York State Exhibit in the Agricultural Building at the
World's Columbian Exhibition in 1893 in Chicago. Powell's mother
was a Quaker reformer who worked in Sing Sing and who labored to
clean up some of the worst saloons. Powell's whole career involved
fruit and institutional innovation, and his first son became an authority on citrus culture in South Africa.[5]

G. Harold Powell was born on February 8, 1872, grew up on the

3

farm, graduated from the Union Free High School in Chatham, and then worked his way through Cornell University by managing a student boarding house while still finding time for student life. He studied horticulture under Liberty Hyde Bailey, who helped choose him after graduation in 1895 to be the Fellow in Horticulture and gain his M.S. degree in 1896.

The same year, Powell married Gertrude Eliza Clark, also in a Quaker farming family, daughter of a lawyer, who had grown up in Cornwall-on-Hudson and Buffalo, studied classics at Cornell, and won election to Phi Beta Kappa.[6] The two were married in the Friends Meeting House in Collins, New York. They moved to Newark, Delaware, where Powell became the horticulturist and entomologist at the Delaware College Agricultural Experiment Station. His researches led to bulletins on cherries, tomato blight, pea canning, the pear slug, quince rot, European and Japanese chestnuts, and the Chinese cling group of peaches.[7]

In 1901 Powell joined the newly created Bureau of Plant Industry in Washington, D.C., as assistant pomologist to study the problems of cold storage of apples. Two years later the Department of Agriculture published his bulletins, "The Apple in Cold Storage" and "Cold Storage with Special Reference to the Pear and Peach." His study of why apples spoiled in barrels was the first United States investigation of the keeping qualities of a farm product. Up to then farmers and the government had concentrated only on production. In Georgia he had shown why peaches decayed in bushel baskets on trains. In 1904 he became pomologist in charge of fruit storage and transportation, working for faster cooling in railroad cars and more complete distribution of cool air in the cars. By 1905, when the Department's *Yearbook* published "The Handling of Fruit for Transportation," the line of his career had taken a decisive turn away from standard Eastern deciduous fruits toward special "luxury" evergreen fruits in the Golden West.

IV

For years Southern California citrus growers had suffered high losses from the decay of their fruit on trains crossing the continent. What caused this? Growers blamed the infertility of soil, poor tree stock, the degeneracy of older trees, weakness in the fruit when picked, damage of some sort in the packing houses, or delays of freight trains. Some took the view that losses of up to twenty-five percent, though exasperating, were inevitable.

In 1898 E. L. Koethen, a Riverside grower, spoke about this problem to Beverly T. Galloway, chief of the Bureau of Plant Industry who was vacationing on the Pacific Coast. Later John Henry Reed, helped by Frank Wiggin of the Los Angeles Chamber of Commerce, began a campaign. Determined to solve the problem, Reed corresponded for years with Galloway, requesting Federal help. Reed argued that the Bureau had the scientists who could do the research and that the growers deserved help because the problem was interstate—the long shipment across a dozen or more states. Finally, in 1903, Galloway sent out Dr. William A. Taylor, the pomologist in charge of field investigation, who surveyed and reported that the problem was indeed serious. The next year Galloway dispatched Powell west and the "Era" began.

Alert, packed with energy, Powell made important connections, especially in Riverside, traveled through the orange districts, cramming his days with first-hand observations. He kept detailed notes, diaries, expense records to go with his low salary and penurious per diem allowance, and corresponded with the Bureau. He took time almost daily to write his wife, at home in Washington with her first two sons.

At once Powell realized that he had walked into a network of prominent horticulturists "anxious to cooperate and appreciate scientific experiments."[8] They were wealthy, confident gentlemen from New England, the Middle Atlantic states, and the Middle West, some retired, some seeking health, all of them used to commanding. They practiced an elegant monoculture, experimented with species and varieties of citrus and with irrigation, soil conditioning, and protection against freezes. As entrepreneurs who owned and ran the orchards they had developed, they responded to Powell's genial personality, his evident power for negotiation, and his "scientific mind, trained to search out the hidden roots of a situation, a practical view point, and the ability to organize."[9] His letters to Gertrude report repeatedly how he sized up people quickly and won them to his way of thinking.

5

The fruit farmers—who called themselves horticulturists in the city directories—shared a common history of fighting railroads, fruit brokers and commission merchants. They had tackled the perennial issue of water rights and set up districts and organized producers' cooperatives. They had faced competition from citrus growers in Italy and Florida. They held themselves together with common interests, economic and social, at churches, chambers of commerce, fairs, a variety of cultural clubs, Farmers' Institutes, and the annual fruit growers' conferences. Together with associated bankers, doctors, judges, and politicians, nearly all with distant backgrounds and connections, these growers constituted an elite in cities like Redlands, Ontario, Fullerton, Pasadena, Santa Paula, Hollywood (before the movies came), and Riverside with its Glenwood Mission Inn.

Powell functioned as the right man in the right places at the key moment in time. His growing perception of this excited all his senses. His hurried yet revealing letters to his wife and sons reflect the speedburning tempo of his life. In his preliminary research and travel, soon mostly by automobile, as in his later visits to packing houses, he had a quick eye for mechanical injury to oranges that let blue-mold spores penetrate the skin. By April 7, 1905, when he spoke at a Farmers' Institute in Riverside, Powell was providing dramatic proof that the growers themselves were the primary cause of decay. E. L. Koethen called the Institute, climaxed by Powell's address, "a turning point in the practices of citrus culture in California."[10]

Powell recommended more careful handling of fruit to avoid abrasions and wounds. Use a glove on the hand holding fruit, use clippers with blunt ends and cut the stems short, take care to prevent fingernail, thorn, or splinter punctures of the skin or bruises from gravel in orchard boxes. He wanted the boxes of picked fruit to cool under the trees all night and to be carried to the packing house the next morning on wagons with platform springs. He prescribed less washing and brushing, none if possible, and smooth, padded grading guides, sorting tables as level as possible. He wanted no dropping of fruit into weighing machines, no swift delivery from carrying belts, no gravity chutes. He insisted on adjustments in overhead sizers and in hoppers and recommended padded canvas hoppers, also smooth, finished boxes and trays free from bent or protruding nails.[11]

Oranges are not pig iron, he said, not objects to drop like cannon balls. Growers needed to pay laborers by the day, not by the box. They needed to buy or build better equipment. Together with his assistants, Powell experimented with packing oranges in boxes to find out which ways led to decay, which did not, and shipped carloads under varying conditions to determine—and demonstrate—which conditions produced sound oranges in New York. With local publicity stunts he reached small, reluctant growers as well as the affluent proprietors.

For instance, Powell went to the Redlands Orange Growers' packing house on March 14, 1907, and together with his men packed six boxes of fruit, wrapped, the lids nailed, as if going to New York. The boxes then stayed in the packing house, until Powell's group returned on March 27, opened every box and counted and examined every orange. In two boxes packed with perfectly sound fruit, unbrushed, decay amounted to 1.1 percent. In two boxes with brushed oranges, free from any noticeable physical injury, decay came to 2.3 percent. In two boxes with tiny clipper cuts and stem punctures, the damage by mold reached 63 percent. A heading in the *Redlands Daily Review* stated Powell's thesis: "Nine Tenths of Decay Due to Mechanical Injury."[12]

For three winters, those of 1906, 1907, and 1908, the Powell family lived in Riverside, joined in 1906 by a third son, Lawrence. Powell and his team continued their field work, extending it to the lemon industry.

V

In the fall of 1908 the Bureau sent Powell to study the Italian lemon industry and to attend the First International Refrigeration Conference in Paris. He wrote regularly to Gertrude in letters not included here since they do not bear on California. They show him growing in self-satisfaction, social sophistication, and in mastery of his field.

In Britain he met "fruit men" and "fruit house men." In France and Italy he met scientists, consuls, barons, and rich expatriates. In Italy he visited lemon farms, often on terraced mountainsides, and also citric acid and lemon oil factories. He spent a day at an agricultural school in Portici, near Naples. Everyone treated him as a "high government official," a status he enjoyed. On September 22, 1908, he wrote Gertrude: "These Italians seem to feel greatly honored that a U.S. Govt. official should have selected them to visit, and they can not do too much to be agreeable."[13]

His letters convey his high interest in the standard sights, historical and architectural, of London, Paris, Rome, and Naples, and for scenery like that of the Amalfi Coast and of Taormina's setting at the foot of Mt. Etna. He made comparisons with California, the state he now identified with. A sirocco blowing near Vesuvius resembled "a regular Santa Ana." A beautiful garden in Messina "was as large as Smiley Heights" in Redlands. In a Neapolitan garden he remarked, "The plants were much like S. California, pepper, acacia, palms and eucalyptus trees, etc." In Sicily: "The Conco d'Oro, a valley leading in from the sea, reminded me somewhat of Redlands." But: "Etna is more beautiful than any of the California mountains." As a Federal scientist, he learned much in southern Italy and in Sicily. "I secured a mass of data that will help in our California lemon work, and I think will eventually modify some of the western practices."[14]

At the Refrigeration Conference in Paris, the U.S. officials and the representatives of the American warehouse industry elected him head of the American delegation. Using his talent to reconcile conflicting interests, he successfully convinced the French officials that the warehousemen must be accepted as fully participating members of the conference. On October 6 he made a speech, illustrated by charts, that attracted international attention[15] and the personal interest of Dr. Mary Engle Pennington, a fellow delegate, an expert on the refrigeration of meats and poultry in the Department of Agriculture's Bureau of Chemistry. The two had not met before. Europe had aroused his sensuous nature and he had aroused hers. They began a prolonged liaison that Powell kept secret from everyone but his wife.[16] (When he asked for a divorce in 1911, she refused.)

VI

In 1909 the Department of Agriculture for the last time sent Powell to California, with a staff of six experts, to continue the studies of decay in lemons and other fruits. His letters to Gertrude continued to detail his activities, ever more strenuous, and his increasing prominence as a public man. He saw himself as "a hot pumpkin." "I need about three more existences to keep all of these things going." Only briefly and formally did he mention the occasional professional meetings with Miss Pennington.

After the period covered by his 1909 letters from California and the West came more publications, "Italian Lemons and Their By-products," based on the 1908 trip to Europe, and the pathbreaking *Cooperation in Agriculture,*[17] which comprehensively covered the nation's crops and products and took up rural credit, rural telephones, and mutual insurance. He said cooperation was necessary to improve farming methods, reduce costs, develop better financial dealings, and improve handling, distribution, and selling of products. The farmer needed group bargaining power.

After leaving Federal employment in 1911, he moved his family to Los Angeles and then permanently to South Pasadena. He served briefly as secretary and general manager of the Citrus Protective League in Los Angeles, using his magnetic and persuasive personality to lobby for higher tariffs and lower railroad shipping rates. In 1912 he became the general manager of the California Fruit Growers' Exchange,[18] a job he held with distinction until his death in 1922. Under him the Exchange became the most famous and most studied fruit farmers' business organization in the world. He joined his horticultural friends in successfully pressuring the University of California to enlarge the Citrus Experiment Station and to establish it permanently in Riverside. He declined invitations to become a member of the University Board of Regents, to serve as dean of the College of Agriculture, or to become chief of the newly created Office of Markets in the U.S. Department of Agriculture.

In July, 1917, at Herbert Hoover's request, he moved to Washington to take charge of the Perishable Foods Division of the Food Administration. The *Los Angeles Times* reported: "Powell in Charge of All Perishable Food. Post of Enormous Responsibility Given to Local Citrus Expert." His scope included dairy products, fish, and vegetables. Second only to Hoover, he developed a firm organization for moving thirty-five million tons a year, worth eight billion dollars, in a complex system of timed deliveries comparable to a huge irrigation project. After the Armistice he helped Hoover with food distribution in Belgium, France, and Italy. Eighteen-hour work days drained and aged him beyond any full recovery of his once abounding bounce and energy, yet after returning to the Fruit Exchange in 1919 he found himself even more prominent and in demand.

He headed a commission appointed by the Governor of California to study American agricultural colleges and propose a reorganization of the University's agricultural college at Davis. In 1922 at the National Agricultural Conference, called by President Harding, Powell served as chairman of the committee on the marketing of farm produce. On January 25 he made a notable address, "Fundamentals of Cooperative Marketing." Great things lay ahead. Liberty Hyde Bailey wanted him to return to Cornell as a professor of horticulture. California Republican leaders talked of running him against Hiram Johnson for the United States Senate. Friends assumed that if Hoover became President he would make Powell the Secretary of Agriculture.

On February 18, 1922, when he was barely fifty years old, he attended a public dinner at Hotel Maryland in Pasadena. There at the table he fell dead of a heart attack. (His widow lived until 1957, when she was almost eighty-seven. Miss Pennington died in 1952 at eighty.)

A month after Powell's death, on March 20, 1922, a long special memorial service took place in the Morosco Theater, Los Angeles. The audience heard impressive eulogies from Charles C. Teague, lemon grower and president of the Exchange; Ralph Merritt, president and general manager of the California Rice Growers' Exchange; and Don Francisco, former advertising manager of the Fruit Growers' Exchange and now manager of the Pacific Coast division of Lord and Thomas. Francisco, who had been a protegé of Powell, said that Powell "multiplied his ability by the ambition he set fire in others. He breathed in their consciousness the spirit of service that was his."[19]

Two officials had come from Washington, Henry C. Wallace, Secretary of Agriculture, and Herbert C. Hoover, Secretary of Commerce. The addresses by the cabinet members in effect evaluated the whole of Powell's career, including the years of his 1904 and 1909 letters.

Secretary Wallace said that Powell's work aided producers, distributors, and consumers. Powell "came to see that some of the most difficult problems were essentially sociological and humanistic, requiring the development of fraternal and mutually just and friendly relations among men, as well as the control of biologic processes of destructive organisms." Secretary Hoover said that Powell, while in charge "of the distribution of a large part of our food during the war," had moved a maximum of food with a minimum use of transportation, showing "qualities of great generalship." Hoover praised "his capacity in conciliation, his great geniality of character, which amid all the opportunities for a thousand frictions enabled him to carry through the whole organization, a certain basic sweetness and kindliness that lifted him through the most terrible discouragements."

A year later, former members of the Division of Perishable Foods placed a bronze memorial to Powell — "Agricultural Economist Public Servant" — in the Entrance Hall of the Department of Agriculture Administration Building. Again Hoover and Wallace came to express their admiration. Wallace said Powell had made perishable produce a new field of research, for he had seen the need for "a study of the entire industry, from the growing plant to the ripened fruit on the consumer's table."[20]

The era inaugurated in 1908 by the plaque in Rumsey's Pachappa packing house had now been finally memorialized in the nation's capital.

R. G. L.

AN EDITORIAL NOTE ON THE LETTERS

The extant holograph letters of G. Harold Powell are in the Powell Family Papers, Collection 230 in the UCLA Research Library. The texts printed here are those of transcripts made by Lawrence Clark Powell.

Letters in the first group, January 23 to March 3, 1904, recount details of Powell's first visit to California. He wrote to his wife, Gertrude, who stayed in Washington, D.C., with her sons Harold Clark Powell (1900–1938) and George Townsend Powell, II (1901–1955). There are no letters for the winters of the following three years, since Powell lived with his family in Riverside. The second group consists of letters from Southern California and elsewhere in the West, March 4 to August 14, 1909.

All these letters regularly express Powell's love for Gertrude and their sons as he sent messages to them, even after his continuing encounter from 1908 on with Dr. Pennington. The 1904 letters catch the impression of an observant Easterner, brimful of life and open to new experience, visiting for the first time the arid West with its drought, dust, irrigated orchards, exotic crops, and astonishing ornamental plants, together with stunning scenery that Powell always responded to. America still had striking regional differences, to which Powell reacted. The letters catch a transition that Powell shared with his generation, the change from horse-drawn vehicles to the automobile. They show an Eastern man in the process of becoming a Californian in outlook.

The letters of 1904 and 1909 bear evidence of haste in writing — some misspellings, wrong names, errors in fact, illegibilities — and of deeper, persistent ethnic prejudices. Like many in his species, he took pleasure in associating with important, famous, or wealthy people — politicos, railroad executives, millionaire orchardists — and in dropping their names. The letters also show that he remained, as in the farm village of Ghent, at high school in Chatham, and in college amid the lakes and forest trees of Ithaca, a regular social being, genial, radiating warmth, who liked to laugh and dance, who was drawn to women as they were to him, who collected Oriental rugs, antique Colonial furniture, and paintings he thought beautiful.

As the months and years pass, the letters spontaneously itemize his growing drive for a larger income, for recognition and success, his growing desire to dress well, to do well or better in Southern California, which he called "a high pressure country." For years he joined the gentlemen in smoking fine Havanas, until 1913, when he quit. "It is n't [*sic*] a nice habit, and I am sorry I began it," he wrote his youngest son, who for a lifetime remembered him as smelling of rich cigars, soap, and cologne.

I leave the letters as Powell wrote them, including his errors in spelling and punctuation. In the footnotes I have corrected evident factual errors and identified most of the many persons Powell names. I have not identified all of those who are sufficiently identified in the letters, such as personal friends, those who figured peripherally in his social activities, or those who have remained names only despite repeated and reasonable research attempts on my part.

I must acknowledge very substantial and continued assistance and encouragement from Lawrence Clark Powell, who first suggested to me this editorial project and who handed to me full authority to give shape to the manuscript. I received generous personal help from Harry W. Lawton, Management Services Officer, Dean's Office, College of Natural and Agricultural Sciences, and Lecturer in Creative Writing, University of California, Riverside. I am notably indebted to Thomas F. Andrews, Executive Director of the Historical Society of Southern California, to the Publications Committee of the Society, especially to John H. Kemble, to Doyce B. Nunis, Jr., Editor of *Southern California Quarterly,* and to Kathleen Jacklin, Archivist, Cornell University Libraries. I wish to thank, too, the staff in Special Collections in the University Research Library, UCLA; the staff in the library at the University of California, Riverside; the staff at the Henry E. Huntington Library; Charlene Gilbert, Archivist, Sacramento History Center; Jeanette Clough at Sunkist Growers, Inc., Corporate Library; Donald McCue, Archivist, A. K. Smiley Public Library, Redlands; Kriste J. Hall, Heritage Room, Corona Public Library; Mary Ellely, Section Supervisor, Special Collections, San Diego Public Library; Bonnie M. Smotony, Secretary, The Regents of the University of California; and Vivian Wiser, Historian, Economic Research Service, U.S. Department of Agriculture.

In addition to the Powell Papers, a rich treasure, and to sources given in the notes, many other works supplied facts or insights, including but not limited to the following:

California Fruit Growers Exchange: *The Story of California Oranges and Lemons* (Los Angeles, 1943)

Chase, Ethan Allen, Scrapbooks, 4 volumes, 1916–1918

Collins, James H.: "The Biggest Marketing Exchange: California's Citrus Organization and Its Manager," *The Country Gentleman,* LXXXI (January 15, 1916), pp. 95–96, 132

Cumberland, William Wilson: *Cooperative Marketing: Its Advantages as Exemplified in the California Fruit Growers Exchange* (a Ph.D. thesis), Princeton: Princeton University Press, 1917

Gabbert, John Raymond: *History of Riverside City and County* (Riverside: Phoenix, 1935)

Holmes, Elmer Wallace: *History of Riverside County, California, with Biographical Sketches* (Los Angeles: Historic Records Company, 1912)

Jacobs, Josephine Kingsbury: *Sunkist Advertising* (Ph.D. thesis in history, UCLA, 1966)

Knapp, Joseph G.: *The Rise of American Cooperative Enterprise, 1620–1920* (Danville: Interstate Printers and Publishers, 1969)

Redlands Board of Trade: *Redlands: A Perfect Climate, the Finest Orange Groves in the State, Beautiful Parks, Fine Residences* (Redlands, 1912)

Riverside Daily Press: "The Mission Inn," Special Supplement, November 22, 1941

Stadtman, Verne A., comp.: *The Centennial Record of the University of California* (Berkeley: University of California Press, 1967)

Sunkist Growers: *Fifty Golden Years, 1893–1943* (Los Angeles, 1943)

Tweedale, Dellene M., comp.: Register of the Powell Family Papers (UCLA Library School of Library Service, 1964)

Weathers, Lewis G., and Lawton, Harry: "75 Years of Citrus Research," Special Citrus Insert, *California Agriculture,* XXXVI (November–December, 1982), pp. CR-1–CR-16

NOTES FOR THE INTRODUCTION

1. *Thirty-Fourth Fruit Growers' Convention of the State of California, Riverside, April 28–May 1, 1908* (Sacramento: Superintendent of State Printing, 1908), p. 57.

2. *Ibid.,* p. 100.

3. Harry W. Lawton and Lewis G. Weathers, "The Origins of Citrus Research in California and The Founding of the Citrus Research Center and Agricultural Experiment Service," (typed ms, University of California, Riverside, ca. 1985–86) p. 33. When interviewed in New York, Powell cited one shipping concern that followed a suggestion from him, spent two thousand dollars, and cut decay by ninety-five percent, saving "thousands and thousands of dollars." *New York Fruitman's Guide,* June 27, 1907. In 1904 the California Fruit Growers' Exchange lost twenty-one percent of fruit in shipment. In 1907 it lost seven percent for a net cash gain of $1.5 million, *Pacific Fruit World,* March 2, 1908.

4. Photograph of plaque in Powell Family Papers, Package No. 1.

5. Extensive source materials on the Powell and related families repose in the Department of Special Collections, UCLA Research Library, in Collection 230 (twenty-nine boxes and five oversize packages). Claribel R. Barnett sums up the life of G. Harold Powell in the *Dictionary of American Biography,* VIII, pp. 145–46 (New York, Scribner's Sons, 1935). Lawrence Clark Powell reveals much about him and about Gertrude Powell (1870–1957) in *Portrait of My Father* (Santa Barbara: Capra Press, 1986), a work that has a fictional outer frame, and in *An Orange Grove Boyhood: Growing Up in Southern California* (Santa Barbara: Capra Press, 1988). G. Harold Powell is a figure in Gertrude Eliza Clark Powell, *Looking Back and Remembering: An Autobiographical Sketch* (Tucson: Privately Printed, 1987).

6. Her professor of Greek at Cornell was Benjamin Ide Wheeler. Her thesis for the B.A. in literature was "A Study of the Noun and Adjective in Shakespeare." Powell's thesis for his B.S. was "The Effect of Food on the Development of Sex."

7. "There were, I think, two publications on peaches which he issued while there that I have always felt were in a considerable degree epoch making." H. .P. Gould, U.S. Horticultural Station, Beltsville, Maryland, to Lawrence Clark Powell, February 26, 1942, Box 9, Folder 6.

8. Powell to Gertrude Powell, January 28, 1904, Box 1.

9. Lester S. Ivens and A. E. Winship: *Fifty Famous Farmers* (New York: Macmillan, 1924), p. 168.

10. *Pacific Fruit World,* April 15, 1905.

11. Esther Klotz, Harry W. Lawton, and Harry W. Hill: *A History of Citrus in the Riverside Area* (Riverside Museum Press Historical Series No. 1, 1969), pp. 18–19. Powell, *et al.:* "The Decay of Oranges While in Transit from California," Bulletin 123 (Washington, D.C.: U.S. Department of Agriculture, 1908), pp. 36, 39; Sunkist Growers: *The Story of California Oranges* (Los Angeles, 1931), pp. 12ff.; J. H.

Collins: "Behind the Scenes Laboratorywise," *Western Grower and Shipper*, XX (July, 1949), p. 28.

12. *Redlands Daily Review*, March 27, 1907.

13. Powell Papers, Box 1.

14. September 29, 1908. Powell Papers, Box 1.

15. On October 10, 1908, Powell wrote his father: "The charts and the facts that a government man could talk with authority on practical questions seemed to capture them." Though his paper was to take fifteen minutes and discussion ten minutes, a volley of questions extended his appearance to a total of two and a half hours. In his diary for October 7 he wrote: "All of the questions were for information, not controversial." Powell Papers, Box 1.

16. Dr. Pennington, born in Tennessee in October, 1872, was the first woman to receive a Ph.D. from the University of Pennsylvania. Her degree was in chemistry. Her career as a bacteriological chemist and as chief of the U.S. Department of Agriculture Food Research Laboratory receives compact summary in *Who's Who in America,* XI (1920–21).

17. New York: Macmillan, 1913.

18. In 1908 the Exchange, after considering "Sunkissed," adopted "Sunkist" as its brand. In 1952 it changed its own name to Sunkist Growers, Inc.

19. The speeches of Francisco and the others appear in the twenty-two-page but unnumbered booklet *G. Harold Powell Memorial, Los Angeles, March, 1922.*

20. Powell Papers, Box 12, Folders 3 and 5.

G. Harold Powell's Letters from Southern California in 1904

UNITED STATES DEPARTMENT OF AGRICULTURE
Bureau of Plant Industry

Pomological Investigations   Fruit Storage Investigations
G. S. Brackett, Pomologist   G. Harold Powell, Pomologist in Charge

Los Angeles, California
Saturday afternoon 3.45 O'clock
[January 23? 1904]

My dearest Gertrude: We have just arrived. I have sent my clothes to a tailor's to be pressed and fixed up and have a few minutes in which to tell you something of the trip. We had a delightful journey. The train was the finest on the Santa Fe and the service everything that could add to the comfort and pleasure of the travelers. There was a diner, buffet smoker, barber shop, six Pullman coaches and one observation car and library. I made the acquaintance of twenty people I guess. As a whole the crowd was made up of ordinary people, but there were quite a few like ourselves that were members of the upper strata of society. General Wade,[1] Mrs Wade and two daughters from Burlington, Vt. were among those that I enjoyed particularly. There were four ladies from Pittsburg and Philadelphia, very delightful people, who invited me several times to their stateroom to play cards. All of them were old enought to be my mother, and possibly might have been had I not had one already, though one Miss Snowden would need to have been called Mrs first. She by the way is a sister of General Snowden[2] who was a minister to Italy and to Greece. She reminded me of Aunt Laura. She stopped at Pasadena and gave me a cordial invitation to visit them at their cottage. So did General and Mrs Wade, and now I wish I had a dress suit. Then there were four people from

17

Lake Mahopac near New York, named Agor. Rather mediocre. Two of them slept in the lower berth under mine and snored vigorously.

I have had my mind opened to the immensity of the country by this trip. One does not realize what a vast domain the United States is and how many millions it can support until he travels across it. Nor do you realize the enormous tracts of desert land that are desert only because they have no water. For two days we traveled across New Mexico, Arizona, and California and saw not a farm comparable to the eastern farms. The villages are miles apart and are collections mostly of mud huts set upon the sand. Through New Mexico the land is rolling and unsettled. It is covered with some kind of low pine, and has a thin covering of grass. It is used for grazing. The people are Mexicans, Indians and half breeds. The adobe villages, made up of one-story rectangular houses, are quaint enough.

The Rockies are very interesting in South Western Colorado, though not as rugged and high as I expected to see them. We were up in the air 7000 feet in going over them. Arizona is well named, and is literally an arid zone. For hundreds of miles you hardly see a house, except a little collection of huts at the railroad. The land though would blossom abundantly if it had water. It is not a waste land by any means, and some day no doubt will support a large population. The mountains are always on the landscape, sometimes very near and are the most wonderful examples of what nature is capable of doing when she feels badly. They are not like the Adirondacks, covered with trees and bushes, but great barren wrinkles of the most complex kind, rising from 2 to 10000 feet.

The most barren country we passed through today, the Mojave desert. This is literally a vast empire, larger than New England and New York with hardly a green thing on it. The sage covers it thinly, but the sands extend to the mountains on every side as one great barren sea. The mountains are always present in every direction. The lights and shades on them as well as on the desert were most interesting. Everything here is fierce, the sun, the sand, the jagged mountains, the gaunt coyotes and jack rabbits and everything in sight. I would like to explore it, but deliver me from getting caught there alone. No one could live there long without water. The mountains are rich in gold, silver, copper and various other ores, and mining outfits can occasionally be seen against the barren mountain.

I was more interested in two great volcanoes miles apart, than any other single feature in the Mojave. These were great round concave black mountains rising several thousand feet from the desert and the black lava extended for miles in every direction from their bases. The lava exists in the form of an ugly broken and cracked mass forming hills and valleys.

Down in the lower valleys where the oranges begin to show against the foothills, the aspect is very different, yet not so unlike the desert in many respects. The cultivated portions are the mesas at the base of the mountains, but the bowl of the valleys through which we came are not irrigated and are dry. There has been no rain since last spring so everything is brown except where the water has been carried, and there portions are only dots on the broad landscape. I was rather disappointed in the general appearance of the valleys through which we came. I had pictured them as luxuriant with alfalfa and grass and other green things, but this is not so now. I suppose the aspect will quickly change when the rain comes.

I must go now, my clothes are here and I want to go to the Post Office. I hope to have a letter from you in a few days. I shall not make plans until Monday when I will begin to meet people. Tomorrow I will do some calling and will probably take some suburban or mountain trip. I enclose two pictures for Clark and George[3] and much love for you and Mother and the children. I wish all of you could be with me.

Affectionately, Harold

HOLLENBECK HOTEL
American and European Plans
A. C. Bilicke

Los Angeles, Cal. January 25, 1904

My dearest Gertrude: I spent yesterday in seeing the city and took in a good share of it by riding over several lines. I have not seen a city so honeycombed by trolley lines as this is. They seem to run on nearly every street and they extend all over the surrounding country for miles. Some of the country lines run the cars a mile a minute.

Los Angeles is one of the prettiest cities I have seen, and its beauty is due to the large grounds and yards around the houses. In the residence sections every house is surrounded with large grounds that are planted with various trees, mostly orange, pepper, eucaliptis and Eng. walnut. The houses are low, many of one or one and a half stories. Green is the predominating color on the houses and on the other buildings and fences. The telegraph and trolley poles are of sawed stuff, straight and painted, so altogether the city has rather a neat and clean appearance. There are many open lots and they are dirty and full of all kinds of signs. On account of the dry weather[4] they (the lots) are very brown and dusty and this detracts from the beauty of the city as a whole. The city is a hustling business town, over 100,000 people, fine blocks, elegant hotels, and real estate agents thick enough to walk on.

The altitude is not over 200 feet. It is hot at midday and cool and generally foggy at night. The chill is very penetrating. The transition from warm to cool just before sunset is very sudden. Every one says it is an easy place to take cold and a hard one to get rid of one. Altogether, I do not like the climate from the little I have seen of it. At Riverside where the altitude is a thousand feet it is much finer, as it is also at Pasadena where the altitude must be 600 feet.

I called three times on Mrs Wheeler yesterday and once this evening but have not yet found her in. Last night I called on Ida Chace. She wished to be remembered to all.

Today I have met a number of men who control the marketing of nearly all of the citrus fruits of California, and several who control the packing. This afternoon I went to Hollyville[5] near here to inspect a packing house. Tomorrow I go again to look over orchards. Frank Rote saw my name in the paper and called this morning. Through him I learned that Ed. Palmer one of my old Chatham friends was practicing medicine at Hollyville, so I called on him. He was delighted to see me and sent me to the packing house with his carriage. I take dinner there tomorrow. He came here three years ago, as he thought to end his days within a year. Now he seems as well as ever and has a practice that brought in $5000 last year. He took me up a canyon road this afternoon when he went to call on a patient, The hills rose a thousand feet on both sides of the road in many places.

Last night I met in the hotel here C. S. Downes, C.U. '96. He used to take Maude Babcock around quite a little. He says Mrs Oliver is at Pasadena and Miss Claypool who was at Ithaca when we were there. A Dr Baker who was at Cornell is there also and Copeland '95 is here in Los Angeles.[6]

Tomorrow I go to call on a Mr Lyon, a large lemon grower at Hollywood, and I understand he is from Columbia County. Nearly everyone you meet here is from the east, and a large proportion from New York.

I will probably be in this vicinity this week visiting Santa Ana, Anaheim, Orange, Fullerton, Pasadena, Whittier and Alhambra. from here. Next week I will probably work from Riverside. My address there will be "The New Glenwood". So you had better write there until you hear to the contrary. It is difficult to lay out a trip in advance from here. I must go to bed. It is 10 o'clock and I am sleepy and tired. Downes has just come in so I will chat with him a few minutes. Give my love to Mother. Kiss each sonny boy for me. I forgot the ostrich yesterday, so I enclose it now. With much love

Affectionately, Harold

━━━━━━

HOLLENBECK HOTEL

[Jan. 26? 1904]

My dearest Gertrude: I have had a busy day. This morning I was out at 6.30 and went to Hollywood again to look over lemon groves. I spent the morning among the trees and at noon lunched with Ed. Palmer at a fine hotel. After lunch I had a great treat in meeting the famous flower painter Paul de Longpre[7] who has a beautiful house and extensive grounds filled with rare plants. Ed. Palmer knows him well and de Longpre showed me dozens of paintings worth from $400 to $1000, most exquisite in coloring and life. Then he showed me through the grounds and wanted me to stay to lunch tonight. It was a great treat as he is a master. Roosevelt paid him the honor of a call while here, and he (de Longpre) presented him with one of his paintings. Since then three have been ordered for the White House. I wish you might have seen the pictures and the house and grounds too.

When I came into town, I went to the Los Angeles Ice and Cold Storage plant with which I have had considerable correspondence.

The manager brought me up town at a clip that made me hold on. His big "red devil"[8]can go about 50 miles an hour.

Tomorrow I go to Whittier south of here and the next day probably to Alhambra. I am beginning to get hold of the problems in the lemon business and will make more progress from now on. The conditions are entirely different from those in the east and the commercial methods of handling the fruit unique. Until these are thoroughly mastered, it is not possible to plan investigations. The business interests have developed so largely, we have to be much more careful in working here than in the east. I feel that I am making fine progress in getting the confidence of the various organizations. The agencies and exchanges are offering every facility for observations and work, and tonight I have invitations from several places to visit their sections.

A representative of the citrous union — the organization that does most of the fruit packing is coming in in a few minutes, so I must close. With much love to all. Hug the boys for me and Mother too on the sly and get them to return the compliment.

Tuesday night, 7.45   *Affectionately, Harold*

————

HOLLENBECK HOTEL

[Jan. 27 ?]

My dearest Gertrude: I am looking for a mule with a charge of dynamite in his foot. I want him to practice on me for an hour. I paid $5.00 for a newspaper today and haven't finished blanking myself for it. This morning I got a $5.00 gold piece in change, and tonight gave it to a curly headed dago somewhere between here and Whittier for a blooming paper that would have been dear at a penny. I'll charge that up to experience and try not to do it the next time. Everything is silver and gold here.

Today I have been at Whittier, 18 miles south of here and go back there tomorrow. I visited some very fine groves in that vicinity. Whittier was settled by the Friends and is populated by them to a large extent. I wish you would have seen the beautiful lemon groves with me. But the oranges are the most beautiful of all. The dark green foliage and the flaming yellow fruit make a striking picture.

On the way to Whittier we passed through hundreds of acres of English walnuts. They are deciduous, shaped like an apple tree. and have light yellowish gray bark.

I will have to buy a coat and vest. The one I am wearing is turning a dirty grey and looks pretty shabby for meeting people. I will have to get a satchel too. With my $5.00 newspapers I will go "broke" soon.

Your letters both came today, the ones written the 21st and the 22d enclosing your Father's. I will write him while I am here. I was very glad to hear from you and the children and Mother. It seems a good ways from home out here. The general inspector of the California Citrus Union has been in this evening and it is now 10 o'clock so I must close with much love and kisses all around.

Wednesday evening   *Affectionately, Harold*

———

January 28, 1904   7.30 p.m.

My dearest Gertrude: I was out at 6.30 this morning and took the trolley to Whittier again where two men met me and drove all morning through the lemon groves. There are about 400 acres around that neighborhood. The lemon groves do not compare with the oranges for beauty. The foliage is smaller, the tree more slender and drooping, and as the fruit is usually green when picked, it does not take the brilliant coloring of the oranges. Lemons are not picked according to maturity but when they reach a certain size, the size differing with the character and time of season. They are then cured and yellowed in a curing house. The only ones that appear yellow on the trees are those that mature before they reach the standard picking size. This year there are more yellows than usual on account of the dry season. I am finding many places where we can be of help to the industry through careful investigations. The people are more anxious to cooperate and appreciate scientific experiments more than any other class that I have met. Tomorrow morning I meet the Directors of the California Fruit Agency, the organization that controls the marketing and distribution of most of the citrus fruits.[9] In the afternoon I will probably go to Alhambra though I may decide to go to Pasadena instead. It is not possible to lay out a trip in advance as I meet people from day to day that cause a change in plans.

My but the country is dry. There have not been 2 inches of rain since last spring. Every mountain and hill and valley not supplied with water is as dry as a road. Thousands of cattle and sheep are dying in some of the counties from lack of food and water. You can have no conception of the dryness of such a country without seeing it. Today the air is very hazy and smoky. It is dust fom the desert. The winds have been blowing at a high rate for several days, filling the southern part of the state with a fine dust that sifts over the mountains.[10]

It is gloriously invigorating in the middle of the day. The sun is warm, often up to 75 or 80. I wish we had some of the dry air in the east. The dust ruins clothes in a short time. Everyone here wears mixed grey goods. My hat has turned grey and my suit likewise. I bought a black coat and vest this afternoon for $20. I thought black would be good at home for speaking and for evening at home. Now I can meet governors and other small fry without thinking of my clothes. By the way, the General Wade I supposed I was talking to on the way out was Governor Woodbury of Vermont. I met him on the street here today and had a talk with him.

You had better address my letter to Riverside c/o "The New Glenwood". I doubt if I reach there before the last of next week, but I will have letters sent on from there. I will be here till Tuesday or Wednesday probably, then go to Ontario for two or three days and then to Riverside. I must close now. Give my love to Mother and hug and kiss the boys for me with a great deal of love to you.

Affectionately, Harold

HOLLENBECK HOTEL

January 30, 1904
Saturday night 10.15

My dearest Gertrude: It is late and I want to tell you something about my trip today. I haven't missed a day writing to you or to the children since coming, and I don't want to establish bad precedents in that regard. Your letters of January 24 and 25 both came today. I was glad to get them and to hear how you all are and what you do each day. It takes just about a week after writing before a letter arrives. I am sorry you did not hear from me regularly for the first week or ten days after I left. I dropped a postal from Chicago, Kansas City and Albuquerque Arizona or N. Mexico, but as I had to give them to the porters I was afraid some of them might not reach you. I hope you have been getting a letter each day recently, though it is likely that two of mine, like yours, may arrive in one day.

I have had a delightful day. I was up at 6.15 this morning and reached Pasadena ten miles away by 8.30. The trolley ride is through a pretty valley, which is quite thickly settled all the way along with fine residences. The track itself is said to be one of the finest in the country. Including many stops the run is made in twenty-five minutes. A run from here to Long Beach, 20 miles, is made in 20 minutes. That's whizzing. Well, at Pasadena I was met by a Mr Ashby, the general manager of the Lemon Growers Assn. He drove me about twenty miles up the La Canada valley where I saw dozens of lemon groves, none too well cared for. I took a snap of Mt Low[11] up which the trolley runs, and one or two valley views. This is a beautiful valley between a spur of the Sierra Madre mountains to the east and some foothills to the west. It is from 2 to 10 miles wide. The water supply is hardly enough to furnish the groves with sufficient water, resulting in a neighborhood that is less progressive than others I have visited. After dinner I called on Mrs Oliver and did not find her in, and then we drove south of Pasadena to Raymond,[12] Alhambra and San Gabriel. Along this route there are some grand orange groves but few lemons, and the country looks thrifty. The groves around Pasadena, as a whole, are not as well cared for as in smaller places as the owners are largely wealthy men who have groves because it is the thing to do, but who depend on comparatively cheap managers to run the places for them.

At San Gabriel I saw the old mission with its bell tower of six open arches and five bells. I photographed it in several positions. It was late in the afternoon, five o'clock, but I hope to get a good negative. One especially pleasing subject is the stairway leading to the choir loft. Overhanging this is a large pepper tree whose branches hang gracefully over the end of the mission. The pepper by the way is the finest tree I have seen here. For grace and beauty and delicate shading it surpasses all of its companions. It has something of the aspect of the weeping willow, but the foliage is smaller and darker, and the clusters of bright red berries give it a lively tone.

Pasadena is a beautiful place. The mountains are nearby, and the views down the valleys are magnificent. The houses are costly and elegant on some of the streets, but like the rest of Southern California, the prevailing architecture is of the low one-story-cottage type. The altitude is about 850 feet. The air is better than in Los Angeles. The dust though — whew how close it does stay by you! I have had to have my old suit cleaned. It cost $2.00 but it was not presentable as it was before.

I thought of you all many many times today and knew how you would appreciate such an opportunity to see the county. I feel it in my — somewhere, that you will see it before many years when I will be working out here possibly for several months. We could take a couple of rooms and move about whenever I was to be in a new place for any length of time. In a year or two more the children will be enough older so that both could get around more easily than they can now.

You might read the letters to Mr and Mrs Fulton some time and send any that you care to to Father[13] as I do not have time to write to the rest of the family. I go tomorrow at 8.30 to Riverside to meet Stubenrauch[14] and back at night. Send mail from now on to Riverside and I will have it forwarded from there.

With much love to all. Kiss the boys and tell them I think of them many times each day.

Affectionately, Harold

I enclose a Eucaliptus (? spelling) leaf. The trees are often 200 feet high with bark that peels off in long strands once a year. This and the pepper are the most common trees. Both are evergreen.

I saw some cork oaks today and a banana in fruiting and in bloom, also fig orchards, prunes, peaches, apricots and I don't know what else. I'll go plumb crazy before I leave here, I am seeing so much.

My dearest Gertrude: Just a word before I go to bed. I didn't retire last night till nearly one and was awake at six, so the Sandman is around. I returned from Riverside this morning by way of the Santa Ana valley and stopped at Santa Ana for the day. The department has a laboratory of plant physiology and pathology there. Dr Pierce[15] who is at the head of it has had trouble with everyone who has come in contact with him and I was expecting some cold storage from him as he had a row with Husmann.[16] Instead, within half an hour after I was there he was discussing his troubles frankly with me, a thing he said he had never done before. He showed me every courtesy, took me home to dinner, spent the afternoon with me around Santa Ana and invited me very cordially to bring you out and make his home our head quarters. He is a high strung man.

Santa Ana is in Orange County. It is a flat town of about 5000 I should judge. The altitude is not more than a hundred feet. The air is moister than in the highlands, and the temperature more even the year around. In most of the higher inland towns like Riverside it is scorching hot in the summer. South of Santa Ana is the enormous celery industry, and all around it for miles the English walnut is planted extensively.

I must go to bed now with much love to you all.

Affectionately, Harold

————————

GOLDSTONE HOTEL
Mrs. M. Wood, Proprietor

Santa Paula, Cal.   February 2, 1904

My Dearest Gertrude: The Goldstone Hotel is the greatest thing I have struck but in some respects is not quite equal to the New Glenwood at Riverside. My room has an elegant yellow wooden bed that cost at least $2.50. The wash stand has three legs and one that may someday grow into fourth. The proprietress is a fine example of the exhilerating affect of the lovely California climate. Like the washstand she has one short leg, and she makes up in other places and would show up with the best of them on a scales. The Petaluma, the one hotel went up in smoke a couple of weeks ago, leaving nothing but this shack to take care of the travelers. Fortunately this is not a tourists town, so the traveler is not greatly inconvenienced.

I could probably have a good room with the manager of the Lemoneri[17] Ranch if I care to go out there, and I got here just at dark and don't like to drop around as though I was looking for a chance to stay over night.

I am here to spend a couple of days at the Lemonera Ranch, the finest thing in the lemon line, everybody says, in California. They have developed the best system of curing and handling the lemon.

To reach here, we go north from Los Angeles about 30 miles and pass through a 4 mile tunnel in crossing a range of foothills. Then one comes southwest through a valley called the Southern Santa Clara Valley. This valley is several miles wide, varying from two to eight or ten. It is planted in spots on each side near the base of the hills with peaches, apricots, grapes, and citrous fruits.

It seems like being shut away from the world to be over here. This is the coast line of the Southern Pacific. Twenty or thirty miles, probably less, to the west is the Pacific, which the road runs close to all the way north. I suppose this route to San Francisco is more picturesque than the Santa Joaquin Valley up which I will go when I finish the South.

I go back to Los Angeles Thursday and to Fullerton, near Santa Ana, on Friday. Saturday I will begin to work towards Riverside and will visit Monrovia, Azuza, Pomona and Ontario on the way, reaching Riverside the middle of next week. I will be in that vicinity including Highlands, Redlands, Arlington, Colton and San Bernardino at least a week and probably ten days. I suppose Riverside will be the most interesting place I will visit as it is right in the heart of the orange belt.

There is great excitement in town. A darky minstrel show has just arrived, an unusual event evidently as the whole population and the dogs appear to be out in the street. Maybe I will go myself as the "mirth producer" is Mr Clarence Powell. He may be the tap root of our ancestral tree.

Tell Mother please I called on Dr Wheeler this morning and

enjoyed meeting her. Nelly Browning from Chatham is in Los Angeles and will be at Mrs Wheelers Thursday night. Julia Angell, whoever she is, is also here and wants to meet me for my Mother's sake. I guess she is one of the people Mother told about before I left. But after hearing a pedigree that runs back a mile and cousins and children and husbands galore, my mind is befuddled.

This is a regular western halfway house. There a dozen boys and men in the room around a stove discussing the prospective "show" tonight. One has seen every ten cent show on the coast, another "ockypied" a box in the Emporium in Los Angeles once with a rich cousin, and another went to another and saw things.

I must stop now and go out and "do" the town. With much love to you and Mother and a hug and kiss for each boy.

Affectionately, Harold

———

HOLLENBECK HOTEL

Feb 4, 1904   10.45 p.m.

My Dearest Gertrude: I have just come in from a call at Dr Wheeler's where I met Nettie Browning from Chatham. I returned last night from Santa Paula after eleven and was up at 6.30 this morning and off to Fullerton. At Santa Paula I saw the finest lemon Ranch in California, 300 acres under the most perfect cultivation, and the entire business developed with the utmost care. Santa Paula, Ventura Co., is in the Southern Santa Clara Valley, through which the Santa Clara River runs. It is a rich valley and beats the world with its enormous production of lima beans, so they say. I hope to show you some good views taken from a foothill above the lemon ranch.

Fullerton is in Orange Co. in the heart of the walnut industry. I went there to see Mr Chapman[18] who has one of the finest orange ranches in the state, 300 acres in bearing. Last year he sold one car in July that *netted* $2800. How is that for a gold brick. That is the product of half an acre of his grove.

He presented me with a box of Tangerines holding about eighty. I

29

wish you were here to help eat them. I have been treating the elevator boys and the clerks in the hotel.

Your letter with the one from Frances[19] and enclosing one to Mr Curtis came this morning and that of the 30th enclosing one from Father and Clark tonight. You can be sure I am glad to get them and would like to have twice as many.

I leave in the morning for Azuza, and will reach Riverside about Wednesday. It looks as though I would not get home before the 15th as I will probably not leave San Diego before nearly the first of March.

I am tired tonight so I will close and try to write more tomorrow. With much love to you and kisses for the children and a big hug for Mother, and as you will deliver them, they are all for you first.

Affectionately, Harold.

P.S. It is raining. Glorious! Second rain since last spring. You cant conceive what it means. They have been holding prayer services: shooting off powder; cussing the weather service and every old thing to make it rain.

———

HOLLENBECK HOTEL

Feb 5 1904

Dearest Gertrude: I am packing up this morning and will start for Monrovia after lunch. I sent in a box by mail a shell purse for George and a napkin ring for Clark.

I bought a business block for you but cant send it this morning. Will try to have it dug up and forwarded on a box car soon.

It is a lovely morning after the shower. It needs to rain cats and dogs for a couple of days before the rain starts vegetation.

This is just a note. It is not a long letter. It lets you know that I am still in the flesh and adding more each day.

Hug and spank the boys for me. I bought a grip this morning. My case overflowed when I bought the coat and vest.

With much love, Harold

My dearest Gertrude: I am in the little cottage hotel you see in the cut above. You will see the characteristic faith the Californian feels in himself and in his locality in the hotel announcement contained in the letter head.[20] They do have frost, fogs and sandstorms, though the town is beautifully situated at the base of the Sierra Madre range which makes the northern boundary to the San Gabriel Valley. There is a magnificent view across and down the Valley towards Los Angeles which is nineteen miles to the south. I came over on a trolley. The San Gabriel valley is one of the most important citrus belts in the state including Pomona, Ontario, Azuza, San Dimas, Monrovia, Pasadena, Los Angeles and down to the sea. It begins I think at Riverside.[21]

The business is not as important here as it is farther north. Tomorrow I go to Duarte,[22] three miles north, and will probably go to Claremont twenty miles farther on to spend Sunday with Mrs Briggs father, Prof. Cook.

It is cold and rainy this evening. Last night an inch and a half of rain fell here freshing the trees and washing a lot of the dust out of the air. The hills and valleys will probably be covered with a beautiful green while I am here as it is likely to rain more. I am very anxious that this be so, as I want to see California as I had imagine it. The raw material is here. All it needs is half a chance to assert itself when a miracle in verdure, I imagine, will be brought about.

The orange trees are a wonderful sight laden with their golden fruit, set off against the rich green back ground. I wish you could see them as you can have no real conception of their beauty in any other way.

In this valley the groves are set along the foothills. It is a dozen miles wide and the basin is too frosty for oranges. In fact the groves extend not often more than a mile or two from the foothills. There may be a rise of a hundred or two feet in a mile, a difference that may make the business possible or not on account of the cold at the lower levels.

I am writing just before supper. After supper I will finish a letter begun two days ago to Father, and write up my notes for the last two days.

31

Tell Clark I was glad to get his letter and that he must write again. He would like to see the oranges and the lemons and so would George.

With much love to all of you

Affectionately, Harold

———

A. B. COOK
Biology Department, Pomona College
Claremont, California

My dearest Gertrude: I came here last night and am spending Sunday with Prof Cook[23] who is Mrs Briggs Father. This is a lovely place at the base of the Sierra Madre range,[24] overlooking the valley to the east and west for miles. This valley I am just getting straight. It extends from above San Bernardino to the coast taking in at its eastern extremity San Bernardino, Highlands, Upland, Redlands and Riverside, and along the north side and centre, Pomona, Claremont, Covina, San Dimas, Monrovia, Pasadena and Los Angeles where it widens near the ocean. There are many other places in it. All are on the eastern end, and towards the middle for two to four miles from the foothills of the Sierra Madre range.

Pomona College has 300 students and would rank with Haverford or Swarthmore. It is the finest small institution on the Pacific coast. ProfCook has the biology. He knows Father and was in the institute work in New York the winter before Father was director of Institutes.

I took a photograph of Old Baldy Mountain[25] this noon. It is a snow capped peak 10000 feet high. I do wish so much you were here to enjoy the scenery and the different experiences with me. Tomorrow I go to Azusa and Covina, Tuesday Upland and Wednesday to Riverside where I will have head quarters for a week or more. You can write up to the time you get this to Riverside and then you can address me at San Diego. I am not sure where I will stop there.

I must close a drop a line to Clark and George. With much love

Affectionately, Harold

Sunday afternoon   Feb. 7 04
Tomorrow I will be 32

32

Ontario, Cal. Feb 8, 1904

My dearest Gertrude: I have just been reading about the terrible fire that is raging in Baltimore. It is hard to conceive of the destruction of its great business blocks, at this distance. Today I have been at Glendora and Azusa. I spent the afternoon with a Mr Powell driving through the groves around Glendora. They extend right up to the Sierra Madre range and down four miles into the valley. Some of the finest groves I have seen were there. At Azusa I looked over some of the packing houses and groves. The Slosson Ranch with 700 acres of oranges and lemons is there, and it is beautiful property. The trees were loaded to the ground with oranges, and the avenues were lined with double rows of palms. I was out of plates or would have taken the palm avenue.

I am at Ontario tonight and will look over packing houses and groves at Upland, which is North Ontario, tomorrow. This is one of the great orange centres. I will go to Riverside tomorrow night and will be there probably about ten days as the towns near there, Redlands, Highlands, Colton, San Bernardino, Arlington Heights are the greatest orange centres in the state. I hope to find some letters from you at Riverside tomorrow night. Some may have gone down to Los Angeles but they will be returned.

Prof Cook has a pleasant house. His first wife Mrs Briggs mother died about ten years ago. He married a few years ago again. His present wife was a minister's widow. He has a beautiful daughter who graduates at Pomona this year. She has a rich contralto voice which they want to have trained in Boston. She gave us a fine lot of selections last night. Prof and Mrs Cook and the daughter Miss Eldridge wished to be remembered to you and said they want you to come there when we come to California.

I hope George is feeling better. The little fellow has had trouble with all of his teeth. I hope you are feeling well too—better than when you wrote last. Give much love to Mother and the babies. I must write up my notes.

Affectionately, Harold

Sunday evening 6.50 o'clock

My dearest Gertrude: I have a few minutes before supper. Stubenrauch' train did not arrive till I was ready to leave so I decided to spend the night. For grandeur and elegance this hotel is ahead of everything I have seen anywhere. It is built like an old Spanish mission with an enormous court surrounded by the wings and the rear of the building. I enclose the plan of the building. Imagine my surprise when the Proprietor[26] asked me to stay as his guest while I am in Riverside! He knew of my coming and takes a great interest in the orange and lemon business so he said I was to have anything I wanted while I am here. Of course I wouldn't accept such hospitality.

The interior is magnificent and the ground, a perfect bower of tropical plants. The Hotel is only a year old and is especially proud of having had President Roosevelt take part in the opening a year ago. The President helped transplant one of the original navel orange trees sent to California by the department years ago. It stands just in front and is fenced in.

I have not had an opportunity to look around any. This is one of the wealthiest towns in California and the very heart of the orange business. I will not return for about ten days and then will be here a week or ten days studying the surrounding country. I met a Mr Reed[27] of the Chamber of Commerce who is to arrange for a meeting of growers and packers when I come. One has to look out that his head isn't turned by the attention everybody shows you. The business has developed on an enormous plan, but little attention has yet been paid to the difficulties. Now that competition is more severe and the troubles increasing, the business interests are ready to spend time and money on any lines that promise to help them.

I can't write more now. I wish so much you could be here. With much love to you and the children and Mother.

Affectionately, Harold

My dearest Gertrude: Your letter came last night with one from Mother, and the Star came this morning. I was glad to get the Star and know more about the fire. I wish I was at home with you today, or rather I wish all of you were here. It is a lovely warm day as all of them are here. The rains a week ago have helped the country some but not enough has fallen to start vegetation generally.

Yesterday I had a most enjoyable day at the Arlington Heights Trust Co property. The general manager Judge Mills[28] took me with a little span of horses in the morning and in the afternoon we drove an automobile. This is the largest orange and lemon ranch in California. There are 1500 acres of oranges and 500 of lemons. I spent all day in the lemon groves and will take half a day in the oranges and a full day in their packing house. Arlington Heights where they are located is about eight miles south of Riverside and from 1000 to 1600 feet elevation. The views from there are grand — over thousands of acres of groves and to the mountains on every side. Old Baldy, Cucamonga, San Bernardino, and Greyback, the highest mountains in the Sierra Madre range are in full view.[29] I took several pictures and got very good ones. I developed them this morning after breakfast. I will have several good pictures of the surrounding country which we will make up in a Blue Book. I have developed three dozen and have two dozen good ones. About a dozen are outside views. Mrs Mills gave me a collection of photos last night showing some beautiful snow scenes on the mountains and some fine cloud effects. These are aristos. This afternoon I am going out for a walk to call on some people with whom Close used to live. Tomorrow morning I go to Highgrove with some growers to look over orchard conditions on the cold lowlands. Tuesday I go to the Arlington Heights packing house. I want to get away by Friday spending two or three days at Redlands before going to San Diego.

This is a great opportunity for me. I feel that my eastern work will be greatly benefitted by the broader outlook this gives me on horticultural conditions in general. The cultivation, methods of handling the crops and orchards, have developed beyond what an eastern can appreciate until he sees it for himself. If some of the same business methods could be applied in the east things would be very different.[30]

35

I had quite a time getting home last night. The mechanic of the Trust Co started to bring me to the city about eight o'clock. He had an elegant big automobile and the way he rushed over the streets made my hair rise. It was dark but the roads were fine and he let the machine out to about twenty-five miles an hour. If we had happened to meet a team it would have had to climb a tree to get out of the way. All of a sudden a tire blew up and the machine shot into the side of the road but he brought it back and to a standstill all right. It took an hour to get the tire off. Then he took me to a car line on Magnolia avenue and waited with me till my car came along. Some one is held up every few nights in that neighborhood so he didn't go until my car came along. There are lots of dead beats around California and they do a lot of robbing. A man lost $75 in the hotel a couple of days ago. Someone picked his pocket while he was standing within a few feet of the desk. I have all of my cash in the safe.

It is dinner time and I am hungry. With much love to all,
Affectionately, Harold

GLENWOOD MISSION INN

Feb 10 '03 [1904] 8 o'clock

My dearest Gertrude: I have had a very busy day meeting different people and this afternoon I met the Chamber of Commerce, Board of Trade and a delegation of packers and growers and gave them an hour's talk.[31] There were not less than ten million dollars invested here by the men present. I felt a good deal of responsibility in meeting these men as they are people of large affairs. I was anxious to present our work in a way to convince them of the value of careful work by the Department, and to represent the latter creditably. The interests here are heavier than in any other part of the state, and the people afraid of a pure scientist. I was greatly relieved when I realized that my talk was along the right lines, and have been spoken to by many since.

The president of the Chamber of Commerce, Mr Chase,[32] who has over half a million invested here, and who I learned was a skeptic up to the time I spoke, said that he wanted me to come here and conduct the work myself, and he was going to write the Secretary[33] to that effect. Tomorrow he takes me for a drive to the highest points here so I can get a general view of the country. I imagine I will be here about ten days and will then go to San Diego. Around this place are 20,000 acres of oranges representing an investment of 30 million dollars. The finest place, and probably the largest and best managed orange business in the state, is the Arlington Heights Co, having 2000 acres. The company is an English syndicate. The President, packing house manager and general land manager, were present this afternoon. The President wants me to dictate my talk to his stenographer, as he wants on file, the general principles regarding the relation of commercial methods to final ripening and decay for use in his business. These things are encouraging to me but make me realize that I have a good deal of responsibility in laying out future work here.

I found two of your letters here last night and received one of the 5th this morning. I had not heard from you since Friday, so I was greatly pleased to find them, and so many interesting things in them. I haven't the birthday present yet and am anxious to know what it is. I am glad you found the extra $10. Look under again and see if you can't find another.

Tell Clark I was glad to get his letter, and I hope George is getting on all right by this time. After tomorrow I will write to Coochs Bridge.[34] With a great deal of love from your united Husband, Father and Son.

Affectionately, Harold

———

Glenwood Mission Inn

Monday night

My dearest Gertrude: I showed them that I was as good as their finest. Mr and Mrs Miller, the owners of the hotel, asked me to lunch with them during the ball last evening and presented me at their daughter who presented me in turn to some of the Riverside Beauties. I danced four times and would have done it more if I had had a dress suit. I could have used it nearly every night. I will have to get one made when I return.

I met Mr and Mrs Yale last night and found them most charming people. Mrs Yale's father was in Lincoln's, Johnson's and Arthur's cabinet.[35] She has been telling me a good deal this evening about the people she has known in this country and in Europe. She played on Lincoln's knee, was a favorite child of Seward and has known really every prominent person since then. They go to Redlands tomorrow and have invited me to come and see them. Then they asked if they might call at the office in the Department. I will try to call when I am at Redlands.

I have been driving all day in the rain. This is the second rain since I have been here. Tomorrow I look over a lot of poor low land that has been ruined by the accumulation of alkali from the seepage water from higher lands. The orange groves have been pulled out and planted to alfalfa. Thursday I hope to finish here. In the afternoon I speak again to the growers and packers, and will go to Redlands Friday morning. I will probably be there three or four days and at Highland a day or two and then go to San Diego County. I must go to bed. I didn't go till 1 o'clock last night. I have an appointment tomorrow at eight so good night my dearest and kiss the boys for me.

Affectionately, Harold

GLENWOOD MISSION INN

Wed night

My dearest Gertrude: This morning I spent in a machine shop studying some of the machines used in handling oranges and lemons. Then I called on one of the pioneers and heard about the early settling of Riverside. This old gentleman knew Father at the World's Fair in Chicago.[36]

This afternoon Mr Reed took me for a drive through the first settled part of Riverside, where the orange business began and which has now gone out of orange growing, with many a tale of woe hanging thereby, the land is now used for alfalfa. I got some pictures there and one or two good ones on the way back to town. Tomorrow morning I go to see a Mr Ramsey living three miles out of town. He is a millionaire and one of the best growers around here.[37] In the afternoon I speak again, and that will end my experience at Riverside. Friday morning I go to Redlands and by Wednesday I hope to have seen both Redlands and Highland and go to San Diego. I will probably not stay at San Diego more than four or five days, and then will start north stopping a day at Los Angeles to see some of the fruit men there again.

Then I will stop at Fresno for a day or two if I go up the San Joaquin valley. If I go up the coast line I will stop at Santa Barbara and Watsonville. If I go up the valley then I will come down the coast to Watsonville. This will bring me home somewhere between the tenth to the fifteenth. I shall stop a day at Palo Alto two or three days at Berkeley and San Francisco.

I am hearing the most flattering comments on the way in which people have been impressed with my way of looking into their industry. Mr Reed said today that no one had come to this section who had commanded so much confidence from the large business interests. It seems that everyone before has been a laboratory man, and it seems to be a revelation to have a scientist who knows the practical side as well as the scientific. I think that the distance from Washington makes a department man seem larger than he really is. Mr Reed wants me to come back next winter and get the work started on the right lines. Maybe I will—then you will have to pack your trunk as I won't come across again alone. Wouldn't it be a fine thing if we could be here five or six months?

I must go to bed as I am tired. Mr Chase gave me some fine photographs this morning showing some views of groves.

Stay with Marian till I come back. With much love to you and the children and Marian and Lee.

Affectionately, Harold

———

GLENWOOD MISSION INN

February eleventh

My dearest Gertrude: I thought of you many times today and wished so much that you could have been with me and seen the magnificent hills and valleys with their seas of orange groves. Nothing I have seen in the East equals the magnificent panorama that spread out around me. Mr Chase, the President of the Chamber of Commerce, and who has done more, it is said, to build up the orange industry around here than any other man, came for me at nine this morning and took me on a long drive through the northern sections of the valley. Then we went up the mountain foothills to a road he has constructed above all the groves and just wide enough for a team. This road extends about five miles. From there the view is simply grand. You look down the valley to Riverside six or eight miles away, and the groves are in one solid mass. The same view appears across the valley, or rather the groves extend as a single plantation across the valley to the foot hills up which the groves extend in spurs. The San Bernardino range is to the north east, the Cucamonga mountains to the north while the Sierra Madre range of which these are a part extend as far as you can see to the coast. It is a miracle, this transformation of a desert country into such a magnificent scene, in about twenty years. Mr Chase wanted to drive with me all afternoon as he said he was having a fine time, but Mr Reed, another business man here, was to come for me at one thirty. We got back at two and I stepped into the wagon and we were off to the south. The views from Arlington Heights over the valleys and to the distant mountains was even finer than the ones this morning. I hope to bring back some good negatives from here.

Tomorrow I begin studying the packing houses. I find today that my talk yesterday was successful in gaining the confidence of the people here. You can hardly appreciate how much this means as there is no class of people in the east who approach the orange growers in intelligence and in large business affairs. This evening Mr Reed said he wanted to arrange for at least two more addresses while I am here. I will consent to one on "Methods of Eastern Orchard Management" but probably not to a second one.

Your letter of the 5th has just come in. I wanted to telegraph you to take a train for California. I have appreciated more this year than I have realized before how hard it has been for you at home so much with little to vary your life. I know I should feel just as you do only more so, as my nature would take me to greater extremes. I do hope, my dearest one, that the trip to Marian's will be a change for the good and that you will feel some better there. The children I am sure will be better as they can get out of doors more every day. I have been away nearly always when George or Clark have not felt well. I love

40

you my precious one and wish that that could make you feel stronger.

If I ever come to California for two months we must plan for you to come too. How much a trip like this would do for you, if we could stay in one place some time! I am finding it a hard trip on account of lack of sleep. I do not get to sleep easily at night and am seldom asleep before midnight and awake by six. This is a high pressure country, and I suppose that meeting so many new people every day and seeing so much that I have to think about keeps my nerves strung up. I feel nearly every night that I could go to sleep at once if I could touch you or feel my hand on Clark or George's little face.

Kiss both boys for me and I send you all the love I have. It is always with you, but I have new supplies all the time. Give my love to Mother and to Marian and Lee when you reach there. Tomorrow's letter I will send to Coochs Bridge or rather Newark R.F.D. *3.

Affectionately, Harold

———

GLENWOOD MISSION INN

Thursday night

My dearest Gertrude: I finished here today by addressing about sixty growers and business men. It was ending in a blaze of glory as they passed all sorts of laudatory resolutions regarding our methods of work and the confidence they have in us. They are going to send them to the Secretary and Taylor.[38] I felt some embarrassment when two or three said that no one of the scientific corps had ever come before who was so well balanced practically and scientifically. I met two bank presidents today and they came to hear me this afternoon. The presiding officer with whom I spent all morning in his orchard is a cousin of Roosevelt, an old neighbor of Attorney General Knox, and was best man when Root was married.[39] He was one who spoke this afternoon about my work here and the confidence we had made. This is not egotistical and don't make me feel that way. It is encouraging to me and I know you want to know it.

I feel that this trip is the most valuable I have ever taken not alone from seeing so many new things, but especially in meeting so many big men. It will make my work easier wherever I take it up in the future—and in time will be worth money to me in a larger salary.

I haven't heard from you in a day or two. You may have sent letters to San Diego, but I will reach there before Wednesday. Mr Miller offered tonight to take off my hotel bill but I wouldn't consent. He gave me a souvenir for you. I am tired so I will close. I hope you are at Marian's and that the change will be a fine thing for you. Give them my love and kiss the children. I miss you very much and wish you were here many many times.

Affectionately, Harold

GLENWOOD MISSION INN

Friday night

My dearest Gertrude: Just a note before I go to bed. It is now 10.30. I have been studying machinery all day in the packing houses trying to discover the strong and weak points of the different kinds of graders, sizers, etc. Tomorrow morning I go to the famous Arlington Heights plantation of 2000 acres. Judge Mills the general superintendent comes for me at 8.40 with his big red devil and we will see some of the most beautiful country around here during the day. The general sales agent of the company came for me before breakfast with his big red automobile and gave me a five mile spin this morning.

This evening I have developed two dozen of the pictures I have taken. Several of them are very good but many are overexposed. I will have the time all right tomorrow.

I am special confidential counsel in a love affair here. Coming out on the cars I met a Dr Dolan and we talked together a good deal in the three days from Chicago. He had been assistant supt. of one of the State Hospitals for ten years and was put out recently. He is not a heavyweight as I soon found out. Tonight he came here to talk over his private affairs. He is a widower with a boy 10 years old, is engaged to a young woman with money which he seems to hold in higher esteem than he does her. Another girl is dead in love with him and he likes her as much as he can. The first one is liked by his parents and friends, the second they will have nothing to do with. Someone has been sending letters to the first telling her the most atrocious yarns

42

about him, how he abused his first wife, drinks, etc. all of which he swears is false. The second wrote him yesterday that she would commit some vast act if he married No. 1 and he is afraid she will. He has some money, and he is afraid if he marries No.1 she will cause trouble if his income independent of hers will not support them in good style. He hates to give up the money of No.1, don't like the idea of his people throwing him overboard if he marries No.2, is afraid that if he marries No.2 people will say the letters scared him off. This is the tangle he gave me. I told him to take the one he likes and who likes him and let the consequences take care of themselves. I felt like punching a lobster who has no more backbone and who looks at marriage as he does. He seems to have taken a fancy to me and says he is coming again Monday night.

Give my love to Marian and Lee and to the boys. Kiss them for me twice each and then spank them. With a great deal of love,

Affectionately, Harold

———

GLENWOOD MISSION INN

Monday night February 15th

My dearest Gertrude: There is a grand ball here tonight, a masquerade affair. A lot of the young folks are around with their powder and puffs and big wigs. Dinner is not yet over but the lobby is getting well filled up with outsiders. The orchestra is making things lively as it does every night. I am meeting a good many of the people here since my lecture the other day, which was held in one of the rooms here, and which has been talked about considerably. I have been known as "the government expert." Oranges are the whole thing here, except the tourists, so anyone who comes here from the government which is 3000 miles away must be a big gun. I am holding up my end all right. Some of the tourists have expressed their envy on seeing me out nearly every day in an automobile with Mr Chase or some other high man. I simply act as though I was used to it and that I am willing to meet the best of them. Tonight I am to meet a Mr and Mrs Yale from Tarrytown, N.Y. Mrs Yale is the daughter of some cabinet officer under Lincoln, and owns a large property in the suburbs of Baltimore which is occupied by Mrs John A. Logan.[40] Judge Mills who took me out Saturday took them Friday and I met them through him. She seems to be rated the brightest woman here. Not a society lady, but an intellectual aristocrat like ourselves. The only difference between us is she has several million and we have several mills.

I received your letter tonight with the drawing of the rat and the cage by Clark. Tell him I'm glad to see how well he draws. I am sorry to hear that Grace has gone off the handle again. What an awful trial her disposition must be when she realizes how much trouble it brings upon her. I hope she has seen the light by this time and is feeling better. I am very sorry to hear of Aunt Laura's illness. I hope I may hear of some improvement soon.

Today I have been in orchards and packing houses. Tomorrow I take another auto ride to the Arlington Heights region and spend a day there in the packing houses.

I must close now. The white wigs and bare shoulders are getting too numerous not to watch and so I will stop and set my eyes. With much love to you and the children and those lovely doves.

Affectionately, Harold

La Casa Loma

Redlands Feb 19 04

My dearest Gertrude: I am in a new place and don't like it. The Glenwood is the finest hotel I have ever stopped at and it spoils me for anything not as good. The Casa Loma is a famous hotel in Southern California, but it is not in the same class with the Glenwood. The dining room is a big barny affair, the orchestra a squeaky, jiggely thing and lots of the people have Roman noses.

I have reached here this noon and met a lot of people. I dont expect to have such a time anywhere else in California, as I had in Riverside. There I met the cream of the orange growers and business men. Here there is no special man to make things meet the way it was done in Riverside. I met a photographer here that I met in Upland. He offered me the use of his dark room and I picked out a pretty mountain scene and a little picture of a double row of pepper trees for you, and he presented them to me. We will have a fine collection, and I will add to the ones I have and give to you as my present when I come home. I'll get only good ones so we will have a pretty book.

For magnificent scenery this is ahead of them all. The Sierra Madre range with the great San Bernardinos and Old Grayback forms the northern boundary and sweep around the east end of the valley. Redlands is on the foothills on the south side of the valley. The valley here is only five or six miles across. The finest groves are at Redlands and Highlands. I will take in Highlands from here as a base, driving across whenever I need to go. I think I will finish both places Wednesday night and will go to San Diego Thursday.

I sent a little box this morning with two Camellia buds. I hope they will reach you in good condition. It is a most beautiful flower. I must close now and do more writing. With a great deal of love to you and the boys

Affectionately, Harold

La Casa Loma

Sunday morning Feb. 21

My dearest Gertrude: You cant imagine how lovely the morning is here. Soft, balmy, clear with flowers, pepper trees, oranges and other growing things filling the air with their perfumes. If you were here today we would take a trolley out on the hills and sit on a high knob and watch the changing moods of the valleys and mountains. Yesterday afternoon I took a long drive by myself and wished a thousand times that you were with me. I drove to the head of the valley about six miles, then took a road up the hill not knowing or caring where I was going. I finally landed on a narrow road above the orange groves and came slowly into town on top of the ridge on which the Redlands groves are planted for miles. The view was grand beyond description. In the valley lay Grafton, Redlands, Highlands, San Bernardino and smaller towns which I could distinguish for thirty miles to the west. At the head of the valley, apparently nearby, but fifty miles back are the two fine old fellows San Bernardino about 10000

45

feet and the snowcapped Greyback father back and still higher. Across the valley five to ten miles the San Bernardino and Cucamonga ranges, north of which are parts of the Sierra Madre, and the horizon at heights varying from seven to ten thousand feet. Just back of the Cucamongas Old Baldy, the highest peak in Southern California shows just the pate of his old white head. He must be a hundred miles north or more.[41] To be where this panorama stretches out in relief before you is a great privilege and I thanked the Lord and Uncle Sam several times, that they had given me the opportunity.

I took lunch at the University Club yesterday noon with a Mr Morrison, President of the First National Bank.[42] He is a hustling young man, an orange grower of the finest type, as well as a good financier. Tomorrow is a holiday, so he will not be busy and we are going to drive in the morning and see different types of orchards.

Tuesday I go to Highlands just across the valley and Wednesday to San Diego where I will stop at the Coronado. I get Commercial rates at the hotels, so I can enjoy the best at a reasonable cost.

I hope you are having a good time at Marian's and that the change will give you some needed rest. Let the children play out doors all they can as it will be a fine thing for them.

Mr and Mrs Yale are here and I have a table with them. They are delightful people. Mr Yale knows Uncle Jacob slightly. He is here for his health and is improving every day.

Affectionately, Harold

LA CASA LOMA

Sunday night Feb 21

My dearest Gertrude: I wrote this morning but I must drop a note to tell you about the grand ride I took this afternoon. Mr and Mrs Yale and Mrs Yales niece, who is the wife of a physician here Dr Whynn[43] and I took a double team and drove first through Smiley Heights, the magnificent park grounds of Mr A K Smiley, who has the famous hotel at Lake Mohonk where the Vandegrifts, Charlie Underhill and others used to go in the summer. These are among the finest grounds in California. I have a letter to Mr Smiley and I may go up and meet him.[44]

Then we took the most magnificent drive for about twenty miles over the backbone of the hills above Redlands. This drive is several miles above the town and through cacti, sage brush, chapparal and other herbage. It was built by Mr Smiley and few other wealthy men and is considered one of the fine drives in California.[45] The road runs through innumerable little gulleys and washes and over the narrow ridges and sometimes on the edge of a gorge. But the views are the most extensive and grand I have seen yet. We could look in every direction over the orange country and into valleys where the water has not been carried, and where there are little patches of cultivated fields of barley and oats running into the canyon like teeth. The country through which we passed and for miles south to the coast range is one mass of knobs and little valleys formed by erosion. These little pockets at the base of the knobs are the barley lands. Sometimes they are a few acres only in extent while the larger areas cover hundreds of acres.

[T]he Sierra Madre extend[s] from near Los Angeles where they spin off from the Coast range around back of Redlands and Riverside. The citrus belt is largely along the foothills from Los Angeles to Redlands and across the upper part of the valley at Redlands and Riverside. All the rest of the country from this valley east and to the main Sierra Madre which run down near the coast at San Diego and here make up the Coast range again, is made up of the most broken type of foothills, with their eroded valleys and benches.

We were up in that V shaped land above Redlands and Riverside. We could see the mother mountains or Sierra Madre for miles, and the foothills of broken country in one direction and the great orange valley in the other. I never had such an outlook as that. Mr and Mrs Yale have added greatly to my pleasure. Mrs Yale has asked to call on you sometime when she is in Washington. She is a splendid woman between fifty and sixty, but very young in spirit.

I must go to bed as I have a big day's work tomorrow. I have just arranged to meet Mr J W England tomorrow. He is a Philadelphia merchant, who has large interests here.[46] He and Mr Smiley have made Redlands to a very large extent. My fame is just getting abroad here, and now the millionaires want to make appointments with me. Kiss the boys for me and spank them both.

Lovingly, Harold

We didn't get home till after dark and saw what they say here is the finest sunset this winter. It was a blaze of the most brilliant clouds and colors.

HOTEL ROBINSON, SAN DIEGO

24th February

My dearest Gertrude: I was so glad to get your five letters from the 13th to the 18th today, the last being written after you arrived at Marian's. It was a week that I did not hear from you and I got pretty anxious for a letter. I am glad that you are at Marians and hope the change will be a good one for all of you, and especially for you and George.

I reached here at noon today and got my first glance of the Pacific, though I haven't seen much of it as there has been a heavy fog all day.

This afternoon I spent meeting people and this evening went over to Coronado to take dinner with Cousin Jim and May Gardiner. They have a large house facing on the hotel grounds. They are overrun with relatives. Jim took me over to the hotel to look around and he said they had been camping on them for weeks. His Father in law, Mother in law, an uncle and aunt and a niece are the crop. He says they dont mind a few for a day but he is getting rebellious after three months. The Gardiners was where I stayed some of the time when I was in Chicago in 1893 and where Harold and I called. They are fine people.

Tomorrow I shall be around town in the packing houses. Friday and Saturday I spend in the El Cajon lemon district about miles from here. I will return Saturday and go to the Coronado[47] over Sunday and make that my headquarters till Tuesday when I leave, or rather leave Wednesday morning for Los Angeles. I will probably be there Wednesday and at Santa Barbara Thursday and Friday. Then for Watsonville and the Santa Clara valley. I will probably not be able to get away from San Francisco before the tenth and will be home by the

15th. I am anxious to be there now and wish the trip was over. I'll hug you to death, half anyway, when I do get there. I don't like to be away from you and the children so much.

Yesterday I was at Highland and back to Redlands in the evening. I left there at 7.35 this morning. Lillian Blainwell was on the train and sent her love to you. She has a very small delicate hand and a lovely eye. I cant say much about this place it is so foggy. We came through one ranch of 104,000 acres this morning. That's farming of a ponderous scale. I saw several eight horse plows in the fields. Monday and Tuesday I shall be at National City. I was sorry to hear of Aunt Laura's death. It will make a big change in the household. I will write Uncle Jacob.

I hope Harold can stay in the Adirondacks next summer so you can go up there again. I will take three weeks with you if possible. Tell him not to worry about the money he owes. He can keep it as long as he needs it.

It is after eleven and I am tired so I must go to bed. With a great deal of love and a kiss for you, my precious one, and kisses for the boys.

Affectionately, Harold

I forgot all about Clark's birthday.

━━━━━━

HOTEL ROBINSON, SAN DIEGO

Thursday night Feby 25th

My dearest Gertrude: I have had a busy day. This morning I looked over some packing houses in town and this afternoon went to National City and Chula Vista to look over a big lemon section that is dying out for lack of water. It was the most desolate citrus region I have been in. Tomorrow morning I go up the El Cajon valley and will visit Lemon Grove, La Maca,[48] El Cajon, Springdale and some other places, returning Saturday night.

I have been with Mr George H. Perkins of Jackson and Perkins, Newark, N.Y. the last couple of days. He is one of the largest nursery men in the country. He knows Father and a good many people that I know. I met him first at the Glenwood and again on the train coming down yesterday. He is stopping here.[49]

I had an awfully funny experience today. I engaged a livery for 12.30 to drive to National City. When I went out from dinner I asked for the rig and the clerk told me it was hitched to a post outside. I went out and saw an old bay horse and didn't like his looks and came back and asked the clerk again. He said it was my horse, so I took it and started for the City where I had an engagement. The old pelter wasn't good for anything and I was mad all the way down and was prepared to give the liveryman h--- when I returned. Everytime I lambasted the horse, he would jump up in the air with his front feet but they would come down in the same place, so he didn't cover much ground. But he got hot and began to lather.

An old Uncle Reuben stopped me and said "Say young man, aren't you driving that hos pretty fast?" I said I hadn't discovered any tendency in that direction, and gave the horse another whack. I expected that he was an officer and might pull me but I kept on—and grew madder every minute.

When I got back tonight an old fellow was sitting on the steps and as I got out he squared up in front of me and said "Are you the man's been driving this horse all afternoon?" I thought he was the liveryman and I told him I had driven the old skate and I would see him in Hades before I would pay him his bill. The old fellow cooled off a little and said something about an outrageous mistake, and then I began to see through things. He said some one would have to pay dear for it and he was going to make trouble. Then I asked him what was the matter and he said when his wife came out of the hotel where she was selling some things her horse was gone. They lived three miles in the country and she ran home and told him the horse was swiped. He got into town as fast as his legs would carry him and made an attack on the hotel. The clerk said he came in like a whirlwind and began to ask questions. He went out with him and they discovered a livery horse standing at the post and then decided I had taken the horse. The old man was wild. He wanted my name and wanted to have me hunted up, and was going to start after me. But the clerk wouldn't tell him who I was or where I had gone. So he paced up and down the walk from 3 to 6.30 waiting for me. In the meantime the liveryman had to get his horse, and I was pushing my old mule and spitting dry all the time.

Finally the old fellow said it wasn't my fault and he didn't blame me any. I told him he ought to have the livery fee, and he said to bring that clerk right out and we would settle it then and there with him or he would make trouble. So I went in and turned around and came out and told him the clerk was out and offered him $1.50, the price I agreed to pay for the livery. He said I was a gentleman and took it but swore at the damned clerk and said it was all his fault, and that he would pay dear for it or he would know the reason why. The clerk and I nearly collapsed laughing and they have jollied me all evening about my trotter.

Every time I think of it, I laugh and laugh as it was a ridiculous blunder. Send this to Mabel as she will enjoy it and she can forward it to Ed and Grace.

I go to the Coronado Saturday night when I return. Sunday I take dinner with Mary and Jim Gardiner. I met a lot of people today with whom I got acquainted on the train coming out, the party of four ladies from Philadelphia with whom I played cards, and the other party, Governor Woodbury and his family from Vermont. All of them asked me to call. Wish I had my spike tail. With much love to you and the boys. Kiss and spank each one for me.

Affectionately, Harold

The temperature at noon today was 75.

———

Hotel del Coronado

28 Feby

My dearest Gertrude: I was so busy yesterday I didn't have time to write. I went to Lemon Grove, Spring Valley, Cajon and Lakeside. These are all in the Cajon Valley which is a beautiful valley about twenty miles long and five or six miles wide. It produces olive, grapes by the thousands of acres, orange, lemons and grain. The mountain scenery is not as grand as it is at Redlands or Riverside, but the whole valley is one of the prettiest I have seen. Lakeside is a resort place. I was there all of today and met several fine people in the lemon business. The industry is not in as good condition as it is where I have been on account of the lack of water and the alkali in some of the water.

I got back here tonight and am watching the fashionables tonight. I am greatly struck with the commonness of the resorters. Crooked nosed Jews, spider legged, redheaded, waspwaisted bent forward girls trying to look Gibson like but looking like a bent pin.[50] This is a high flying place I judge. It is a magnificent, massive hotel, the second largest in the country. But it doesn't compare with the Glenwood for artistic finish and homelike comfort. I pay $4.00 a day for a small coup of a room with a folding bed.

I will be here till Tuesday, when I go to Los Angeles. Thursday morning I leave for Santa Barbara and will be there a day, then go to Watsonville, reaching San Francisco about Tuesday. I hope to leave for home by Thursday, reaching there the following Tuesday. I will be so glad to get back again and see you and the children.

Tomorrow I take dinner with Jim and May Gardiner who have a big house facing the grounds. The hotel here is on a peninsula across from San Diego.

The Bay is said to be the finest in the country. That is, it makes the finest harbor in the country. The climate is better than Riverside — more uniform and softer on account of the ocean. The country dont begin to be as well developed or as beautiful.

Later 11 p.m. I met the four Philadelphia and Pittsburg Ladies and they inveigled me into playing cards. I played with Mrs McCune the mother of the first vice president of the Carnegie Steel Co. and we beat every game. After that I took the younger ones, the youngest about 40, to the ball room and there danced two hours with some girl. She is a sister of General Snowden of Philadelphia who was a minister to Greece and to Spain. I had a pleasant time as they are delightful people. Miss Snowden, though old enough to be my auntie, is as light a dancer as many of the younger set with roses still on their cheeks.

I am sleepy and tired so I must close with a great deal of love.
Affectionately, Harold

Dear Little Boys: I saw a big pelican tonight when I came across the bay on a boat. He was sailing in the air looking down on the water to see a fish, which he wanted to catch for his dinner. All of a sudden he saw one and shot down head first and went under the water. When he came up he had a fish in his bill and he swallowed it. Wouldn't you like to see him do that? When I come home I will tell you about it if you will remember and ask me. With much love and a kiss

Papa

HOTEL DEL CORONADO

28 Feby

My dearest Gertrude: I have had a fine day. This morning Jim Gardiner came for me and walked about two miles down the beach along the ocean. Then we took a stroll over the golf links where Jim is the champion of the Pacific coast. Paul, the oldest boy, 16 years, is the juvenile champion, and the champion juvenile tennis player of the U.S. Paul and a girl are the champion mixed players, and Jim plays in a mixed tournament tomorrow with a champion woman player, for the championship of the coast for mixed players. You would enjoy the Gardiners very much. They have a good deal of money but are unaffected by it.

I am going to dinner with them again tomorrow night. They wanted me to stay with them, but the house is full and I feel more comfortable here. Down on the beach this morning were hundreds of thousands of gulls. They made acres they were so thick. They are scavengers as well as fishermen. There were also quantities of snipe.

The flowers here are enormous. The aurancarias,[51] like the little one we had, are 40 feet hight. The Hibiscus plants are small trees 10 or 12 feet hight. Geraniums are several feet high and cover a large space. The acacias, which we have in pots are shade trees and the palms are big enough to build a small house under.

A number of people have come in today whom I have met at different parts of my trip. Everybody gets acquainted out here.

I must go to bed. With a good deal of love,

Affectionately, Harold

1st March

My dearest Gertrude: I have just had a delightful call on Mr Smith Thompson, President of the First National Bank, Hudson. He knew Father and Mother and good many that I know. I saw his name on the register and looked him up. He was very appreciative of the compliment. Mrs Thompson had retired so I missed seeing her. I was at dinner with the Gardiners tonight. I like them ever so much. May and Jim both sent regards to you and invited us to come to Chicago and stay with them if we ever come in that direction.

I have had a busy day driving through a desolate country where the lemon business has been badly injured by the short water supply.

I suppose your letters are going to Berkeley now. I have had none since the installment when I arrived. I will write Dr Hilgard[52] and ask him to send them to Watsonville as it will be a week before I reach San Francisco. I will leave Los Angeles for Santa Barbara Wednesday afternoon and will probably stay there till Friday afternoon. Then go to Watsonville and San Cruz.

I am awfully tired and sleepy and must go to bed. Kiss the boys for me. I hope they keep well and that you are feeling better on account of the change. I will reach home about the 15th to the 17th and will be glad.

Affectionately, Harold

2d March 1904

My dearest Gertrude: I am back at Los Angeles again and wish now that I would start direct for home. I am not going to be here so very long and want to start east within a week. I leave in the morning for Watsonville and will be there Friday and Saturday. I would like to spend Saturday night with Prof Roberts at Palo Alto if I could get as far north as that. Monday and Tuesday I will be in Berkeley and San Francisco and will probably start for home sometime Wednesday, reach Washington the following Monday or Tuesday. I will return over the Denver and Rio Grande as that is the finest scenery. You go up 11 or 12 thousand feet.

I have been busy here this afternoon. I met Mr Perkins again here, and Mr Chase at Riverside who did so much for me is here also. I have made lots of friends among the orange and lemon people.

A number of them want me to come back next year and start the work even if I don't carry it on. The trip has been worth a good deal to me in a good many ways. I don't believe I would care to spend much time on citrus problems but would rather work with the deciduous fruits. I would like a season in the apple districts of Colorado, California, Oregon and Washington.[53]

I got two more coffee spoons today, one a Coronado and the other a San Gabriel Mission spoon. We will have to get a set of coffee cups now to match the spoons. I am too tired to write so I will stop. I have been waking up early every morning, about five to half past, so I am sleepy. Kiss the boys for me and with much love to you and Marian and Lee.

Affectionately, Harold

━━━━━━━━

PALACE HOTEL
San Francisco

March 3 1904

My dearest Gertrude: I reached here this morning at 8.45 after sitting in the moonlight last night with a good looking young lady physician from Detroit. A lot of us sat up until after we passed through the Tehatchapee pass[54] and around the loop. There is where the Coast range and Sierra Madres meet and where the train climbs into the San Joaquin valley from the south. It was great—especially the doctor—she graduated at the U. of M. in 1898 and was very lovable and sweet. I couldn't leave her alone, that wouldn't have been upholding our family traditions, and I couldn't very well ask her to go in, and leave me out there alone. I told her I had nine children and that my wife had over half a million in her own name. Otherwise she might have made some plans of her own. I never could keep the girls away. There's no use beginning this late.

55

Everything up here is soaking wet, even the bay, which I have crossed three times today. The rains have been very heavy and the Sacramento has been cutting up all kinds of stunts in the bejoyful overflowing line. Thousands of acres are under water along the river banks. If they could only distribute some of the moisture in Southern California it would relieve them here and save them there.

I haven't seen much of San Francisco. It has been very foggy and rainy all day. I went over to Berkeley this afternoon and met Stubenrauch. His mother in law decided to die just after I reached there and he left hurriedly for Sacramento. I met Dr Hilgard the Director who has been attacking Whitney[55] so savagely and lately has let his vitriol spread over the Secretary. He has also had a whirl with Husmann. Stubenrauch and others I met first prepared me for an outburst from the Doctor, so I put on my diplomatic gloves when I went in, and instead of arousing the old gentleman, I soon had him in a garrulous mood and he kept me from 3 to 5.30.

About 4.30 I led up to the Department and then asked him frankly what the trouble was from his point of view. He told me in the most dispassionate way without getting at all excited all about the difficulties that he has been attacking. I learned what I suspected, that a good deal of Whitneys and Husmanns faults were due to their arrogant personal methods and they had not dealt with the Doctor and his work in the spirit that makes people feel good. He is over 70 and has been working 50 years as a chemist. He is out of touch with modern education and has not built up the College of Agriculture and the Secretary has jumped him no harder than a young man would deserve, but the Doctor, being a Dutchman, such treatment makes the hair stand out all around his neck, and then he gets out his pen and says things. I am going back in the morning to see him again as he asked me especially to meet his staff. I couldn't have been treated more courteously, and he said he was very glad we were going to take up the lines of work I outlined to him.

Yesterday a delegation came down to Los Angeles to talk over the needs of the Horticultural interests in Southern California from the educational standpoint with me. I spent four hours with them outlining what they would have to do to get the State behind them. Our great trouble here is that Dr Wheeler,[56] like Schurman a few years ago, is not in favor of building up Agriculture, and with Hilgard, like

Roberts,[57] at the head of the College and Station, there is little hope of getting things changed easily.

Here is the next and best news. I have my ticket and sleeper for Sunday morning. I leave here at 10 a.m. and reach Chicago Wednesday night about 9 p.m. There are no more trains that night so I leave at 10 a.m. Thursday morning and will be in Washington Friday afternoon sometime about 3 or 4 o'clock. So come down Friday and we will have a big family reunion Friday night. If for any reason my train should be late and I should be delayed a day, I will wire you at Washington sometime Friday. Don't get the childrens hopes too high for Friday as there might be some delay from snow in going through the mountains. I go to Salt Lake City and have five hours there, then over the Denver and Rio Grande—the most magnificent scenic route in the country.

With much love

Affectionately, Harold

NOTES FOR THE LETTERS OF 1904

1. Not James A. Wade, a major-general in the Mexican and Civil wars. Five days later, on January 28, Powell correctly identifies him as Urban A. Woodbury, Ex-Governor of Vermont.

2. Archibald Loudon Snowden of Philadelphia served under President Benjamin Harrison as minister to Greece, Romania, and Serbia, and later to Spain.

3. Clark and George are his first two sons. Mother is Powell's mother, Marcia Rebecca Chace Powell, who often stayed in Washington with Gertrude and the boys.

4. In 1903–04 rainfall in Los Angeles totaled 8.72 inches, a contrast to the year before, 19.32 inches, and the year following, 19.52 inches.

5. Powell soon gives this agricultural suburb its correct name: Hollywood. Powell and his friend there, Dr. Ed. Palmer, attended Chatham High School together.

6. Charles Sawyer Downes worked at the University of California. Edith Jane Claypole, M.S., Cornell, 1893, M.D., University of Southern California, was a pathologist in Pasadena and Los Angeles. This Dr. Baker was probably Eugene Baker, B.S., Cornell, 1878, an obstetrician and gynecologist. Clement Austin Copeland held the degree of Mechanical Engineer in Electrical Engineering and worked as a consulting engineer in Los Angeles.

7. Paul de Longpré, a painter of floral arrangements, had his studio in his two-story wooden castle with towers and flagpoles, amid elaborate gardens at the northwest corner of Cahuenga and Hollywood boulevards.

8. Possibly a Pierce Arrow.

9. The California Fruit Growers' Exchange.

10. Powell learned to call these winds Santa Anas.

11. A broad-gauge urban trolley ran from Pasadena to the mouth of Rubio Canyon; then an inclined railway ran abruptly up to Echo Mountain House, from which a narrow-gauge trolley led to a tavern below the summit of Mount Lowe.

12. Raymond, a settlement at a trolley stop between Pasadena and South Pasadena.

13. George Townsend Powell.

14. Arnold Valentine Stubenrauch, an assistant professor of horticulture at the University of California and superintendent of sub-stations. He worked with Powell as an expert in fruit transportation.

15. Newton B. Pierce, pathologist and Director of the U.S. Department of Agriculture Pacific Coast Laboratory in Santa Ana.

16. G. C. Husmann, a U.S. Department of Agriculture pomologist in charge of Viticultural Investigations.

17. Limoneira Ranch, a model agricultural enterprise, later the largest lemon orchard on earth, managed by Charles C. Teague.

18. C. C. Chapman, a pioneering leader in the orange industry in Orange County. Known as "The Father of the Valencia Orange Industry." In 1906 he had become the first president of the Citrus Protective League of California.

19. Frances Hurd, a family friend in Newark, Delaware.

20. The letterhead says, "The Most Healthful Spot in California Is/Monrovia/ The Gem City of the Foothills/On the Southern Slope of the Sierra Madre Mountains/16 Miles from Los Angeles/No Asthma, No Bronchitis, No Rheumatism/ No Frost, No Heavy Frost, No Sandstorms/Purest of Mountain Spring Water."

21. Powell unduly enlarges the San Gabriel Valley. Los Angeles is west of it (in what for a time was called the Los Angeles Valley). Pomona and Claremont are in the Pomona Valley. Riverside, Redlands, and San Bernardino are in the San Bernardino Valley. In Powell's day, as in 1990, the term *valley* is often geographically imprecise.

22. Duarte is east of Monrovia.

23. A. B. Cook, professor in the Department of Biology, Pomona College, conducted Farmers' Institutes in Southern California. He had worked with Powell's father when Powell senior was superintendent of the New York Farmers' Institutes. According to Cook, Powell asked Cook what was the most important problem to be solved in citrus orchards.

"I answered that it was undoubtedly 'greater care in picking and handling the fruit.'

"Professor Powell said at once: 'I believe you are wholly right. . . . We have found the same thing in the marketing of fruit in the East.'" *Pacific Fruit World,* March 12, 1904. Cook told Powell how C. C. Chapman in his Placentia orchard handled the fruit from the tree to the car "as if it were a tender infant."

24. A popular name for the San Gabriel Range, since 1927 officially the San Gabriel Mountains.

25. Old Baldy Peak is Mt. San Antonio.

26. Frank Augustus Miller (1858–1935), a native of Wisconsin, a Riverside booster and businessman who developed and gained national fame for the Glenwood Mission Inn. On March 14, 1909, The *Riverside Enterprise* quoted him: "The best crop in California is the tourist crop."

27. John Henry Reed (1833–1920), a retired school superintendent and drygoods merchant from Mansfield, Ohio, became an orange grower, actively led in carrying on local experiments to protect orchards from freezes. He led, too, in persuading the Department of Agriculture to send Powell and others west to study the decay of picked oranges. He repeatedly spoke or wrote in support of Powell's findings. Harry Lawton emphasizes Reed's importance in "The Man Who Founded the Citrus Station," *University of California Riverside Magazine,* V, (Winter, 1987), pp. 26–38.

28. James Mills, a justice of the peace, was superintendent of the Land Department of the Arlington Heights Fruit Company.

29. San Bernardino Peak (10,624 feet in elevation) and Greyback or Mt. San Gorgonio (11,502) are in the San Bernardino Mountains.

30. On February 3 in Santa Paula he wrote his father: "The people are far ahead of the easterners in their methods, but they need education all along the line to bring about any real improvements." He said that no one single remedy could help an industry, but the growers want "a precription that in one magic moment will drive away all the troubles and make lemon growing as good as a gold mine. When they reach that stage of evolution that their lemons are grown on beds of roses, the fruit picked by fairy angels and shipped by a Marconi message, they may realize their dream." Powell Papers, Box 2, Folder 4.

31. In his talk, introduced by Reed, Powell complimented the West and California and said his mission was more to learn than to instruct and lead. Agricultural problems found elsewhere were probably here, too. The more rapidly fruit grows and matures the less it has keeping qualities. Factors in decay: the maturity of fruit when handled for shipping, moisture, temperature. Rough handling is bad. "Fruit is a living organism and must be treated as such." *Riverside Enterprise,* February 11, 1904.

32. Ethan Allen Chase (1832–1921), born in Maine, became a member of a big nursery company raising roses, in Rochester, New York, and later became a lemon and orange grower in Corona. With his sons and others he organized the National Orange Company of Riverside, the world's largest orange ranch, 3,000 acres: "Capital $800,000.00 Fully Paid." The Chase Rose Co. of Riverside, wholesale growers, had "Capital $25,000." Chase provided a laboratory for Powell and his fellow scientists. Powell Papers, Box 1, Folder 1; Holmes, p. 564; *Eightieth Birthday Ethan Allen Chase, Chase Plantation, Corona, January 18, 1912* (Riverside, 1912).

33. James Wilson ("Tama Jim"), Secretary of Agriculture for sixteen years under McKinley, Roosevelt, and Taft, revolutionized his department, moving it actively into varied research activities, including the Bureau of Plant Industry, founded in 1901.

34. Coochs Bridge, Delaware, home of Gertrude's sister, Marian I. Clark, her husband Levi ("Lee") Cooch, and their daughter, Margaret. Lee, descendant of one of "the old Southern families of Newark and Coochs Bridge," ran a farm at Coochs Bridge and commuted to Philadelphia to work on a farm paper.

35. Mrs. Yale's father, Hugh McCulloch, served as Lincoln's third Secretary of the Treasury, Johnson's only Secretary of the Treasury, and Arthur's third. The Yales were residents of Tarrytown, New York.

36. Powell's father was in charge of the New York State exhibit in the Agricultural Building at the Chicago World's Columbian Exposition of 1893.

37. Cornelius Earle Rumsey, a prominent grower, was a native of New York who moved west, with stays in Pittsburgh and Chicago, where he served as treasurer of the National Biscuit Co. In Riverside he was active in the Presbyterian Church, the Chamber of Commerce, and the Y.M.C.A. His grove, a showplace, shipped under the label "Alta Cresta."

60

38. Dr. William A. Taylor, U.S. Department of Agriculture Pomologist in Charge of Field Investigations, Powell's immediate superior in the Bureau.

39. Philander C. Knox, Attorney-General under McKinley and Roosevelt, 1901–04. Elihu Root, Secretary of War under McKinley and Roosevelt, 1899–1904.

40. Mary S. Logan, widow of John A. Logan, a general in the Civil War and later a senator.

41. Greyback, not Old Baldy, is the highest peak in Southern California. Powell was more nearly 40–45 miles from Old Baldy.

42. F. P. Morrison developed water and orange groves and established what became the First National Bank of Redlands. John Brown, Jr., and James Boyd: *History of San Bernardino and Riverside Counties,* (Chicago: Western History Association, 1922), III, p. 1253.

43. Dr. Sydney Wynne, physician and surgeon.

44. Albert K. Smiley, capitalist, one of a pair of twins born in Maine who established in 1869 Mohonk Mountain House, "a family resort," on Lake Mohonk, near New Paltz, New York.

45. "The view from Smiley Heights, Prospect Park, and Cañon Crest Park brings irrepressible exclamations from even the most apathetic visitor." Redlands Board of Trade: *A Statement of Facts Concerning Redlands, California* (Redlands, 1905?), p. 9.

46. Thomas Y. England, who was in the wholesale leather business in Philadelphia, owned property in Redlands, including a parklike estate. His son, Dr. James William England, was a Redlands property owner and orange grower.

47. Hotel del Coronado.

48. La Mesa.

49. In a letter to his father on February 28. 1904, Powell said of Perkins: "He handles a large amount of prunes and other California products and grows millions of roses for the eastern trade." Powell Papers, Box 2, Folder 4. Eventually Perkins bought Chase's interest in the Chase Bros. Nursery.

50. In the February 28 letter to his father, Powell said, "There are a thousand people in this hotel but I dont find any that are any better than I am. Its not my fault that I had an aristocratic Father & Mother."

51. The genus Araucaria includes monkey puzzles, bunya-bunyas, and Norfolk Island pines.

52. Eugene Woldemar Hilgard (1833–1916), a native of Bavaria, a geologist, chemist, and pioneer in soil science, including soil physics. During 1888–1906 he was Director of the Agricultural Experiment Station in Berkeley.

53. "The apple is preeminently the National fruit in the commercial pomology of the United States." Powell: "Relation of Cold Storage to Commercial Apple Culture," *U.S.D.A. Yearbook, 1903,* p. 225.

54. Powell's phonetic spelling catches the pronunciation of Tehachapi, printed with variants into the twentieth century. Powell uses the name Sierra Madre as the

Spanish and Mexicans did, to cover a number of ranges. The Tehachapis join the Coast Range and the Sierra Nevada.

55. Milton Whitney, a soil physicist in the U.S.D.A. "The Secretary," James Wilson. According to the *Dictionary of American Biography,* Hilgard, though often "cheerful and vivacious," could show "fighting qualities when sufficiently aroused."

56. Dr. Benjamin Ide Wheeler, President of the University of California from 1899 to 1920. Wheeler had been Gertrude Clark Powell's professor of Greek at Cornell.

57. Jacob Gould Schurman was president of Cornell University, 1892–1920. Isaac Phillips Roberts was dean of the New York State College of Agriculture at Cornell, 1874–1903.

John Henry Reed, the prime instigator

Ethan Allen Chase (1832–1921)

G. Harold Powell, undergraduate, Cornell University, around 1893.
Source: Powell Papers, UCLA Special Collections

G. Harold Powell and Gertrude Clark Powell with sons Clark and George, Washington, D.C., 1902. Source: UCLA Special Collections

GLENWOOD MISSION INN
RIVERSIDE, CAL.

Mar. 3, 1909.

My dearest Gertrude:

VAN NUYS HOTEL
LOS ANGELES, CAL.

M.M. POTTER, PROPRIETOR.

THE POTTER
SANTA BARBARA, CAL.

M.M. POTTER, MANAGER.

Los Angeles, Cal.

My dearest Gertrude:

San Diego & yester-
is leaving The
last night and
Fullerton, orange
now or have

before last about

No. 1.

Hollenbeck Hotel.
AMERICAN AND EUROPEAN PLANS.
A.C. BILICKE

No I.

Los Angeles, Cal. January 2d 1904

My dearest Gertrude:

I spent
city and took in a goo
over several lines. I h
so honeycombed by
They seem to run o
and they extend all
country for miles.
run the cars a mile

Los Angeles in
I have seen, and it

HOTEL HAYWARD
SPRING & SIXTH STS.
LOS ANGELES

THIS HOTEL IS ABSOLUTELY FIRE PROOF
H.C. FRYMAN, PROPRIETOR

March

My dearest Gertrude:

Woodford is coming to

Letterheads for correspondence from California, 1904, 1909.
Source: Powell Papers, UCLA Special Collections

G. Harold Powell, 1906. "The apple is preeminently the national fruit . . . of the United States." Source: Powell Papers, UCLA Special Collections

Part of the California work force in 1907. Rear row, left to right:
Powell, H. M. White, Stubenrauch. Front row, left to right:
Eustace, Dennis. Source: Powell Scrapbook in Package No. 1,
Powell Papers, UCLA Special Collections.

Among the laborers are found Americans, Japanese, Mexicans, Chinese, and a few of other nationalities. Experience has shown that the ability of the labor foreman is of more importance than the nationality of the crew in securing efficient work and that the general policy of those who employ the labor in respect to the care with which the fruit is to be handled is of greater importance than both.

PICKING CITRUS FRUITS.

In picking citrus fruits it is necessary to sever them from the branches with sharp clippers or shears. The fruit is then placed in a picking bag holding from 20 to 50 pounds, slung over the neck and shoulders of the picker. From this it is emptied into picking or lug boxes, and in these the oranges are delivered to the packing house. Sometimes the packing or shipping boxes are used for this purpose once before s h i p m e n t. Formerly the most common type of shears in use was a small one with s h a r p-p o i n t e d, c u r v e d blades, shown in figure 1, A, which, when

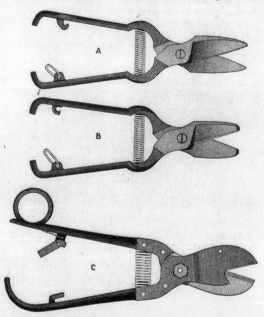

FIG. 1.—Types of shears or clippers used in picking citrus fruits. A, a sharp-pointed type; B, clippers with blunt points; C, sheath clippers.

not handled with care, often punctured or cut the skin of the orange. Since greater care and attention have been given to the operation of picking, many new styles of clippers have been invented and put into use, most of them with rounded or blunt points. Blunt-pointed clippers are shown in figure 1, B, and another style, known as sheath clippers, in figure 1, C.

123

A page from U.S.D.A. Bureau of Plant Industry Bulletin 123 (1908)

G. Harold Powell, 1912

George Townsend Powell and G. Harold Powell, father and son, 1918.
Source: UCLA Special Collections

G. Harold Powell's Letters from California and the West in 1909

HOTEL HAYWARD, LOS ANGELES

March 4, 1909

My dearest Gertrude: Woodford[1] is coming to lunch with me in a few minutes. I have tried to write for a day or two but have been on the jump. Tuesday I went all over the Highgrove district with Harry Chase[2] in his auto. In the afternoon Lyman Brown[3] took Mr Chase, Harry, Frank[4] and I to Corona. We had lunch at Harry's. I called on Miss Handy[5] Monday. It seemed strange enough not to have you there. We lived 2 years altogether in her house. When I go up or down the street it seems as though I would see you coming out of some store with the baby.[6]

I have a room at the Glenwood in the annex. 1.25 a day and 75 cents for each meal. I pay only for those I have. Mr Miller was glad to have me stay there and said I could make my own price and keep a record of all meals. I have a quiet room and hope to sleep better from now on. I have been waking too early, 4.30 and 5.00 and I get rather tired. For 2 nights now I have slept till 6 or 6.30.

Stuby[7] came to see me Sunday night and stayed till Tuesday. Monday evening I was invited to a very exclusive affair — a birthday party for Miss McDuffy. She is the reigning belle at the Glenwood, a very talented elocutionist and all around woman. Dr and Mrs Wilson and Anna[8] were there — about 20 of us in the adobe. I'm as good as the best and I am glad to have them recognize merit when it is around. Tonight I am to dine with the Wilsons and tomorrow afternoon I take Mr Chase's team and take the Wilsons around Eureka. I have a bag of Eurekas in my room.[9] I will send you a box of them a little later.

I came down here yesterday afternoon and went to Pasadena at the Ice House where the boys were examining fruit. We all had dinner here last night. I go back to Riverside at 3.30. I forgot to figure Josh's check.[10] I deposited $300 along the last of December. You will find the date of deposit in the stubs of the checkbook. I think it is in a detached stub. You can send Josh a check the middle of March or April 1st or April 15th. Figure the number of days at 6 %.

I sent in an expense act of $45 a few days ago. Send the check to Father after you endorse it. All the expense account checks must go to him till we pay $150.

I am not spending much on myself here. I bought a soft hat — green and will get a suit later. Tell the boys I wish they were here. I miss them and you very much. I wonder what kind of day you are having. I saw in this morning's paper that yesterday was a very bad day and that the streets were full of slush.

I wish you could make a couple of dollars a day on a room. You could have something nice with the money. I am glad you have the dishes. I will be in San Diego County most of next week. Mail can go to the Glenwood just the same.

Our work never stood better out here. With love and kisses to all of you

Affectionately, Harold

Riverside March 5, 1909

My dearest Gertrude: Taylor made the first mistake I ever knew him to make. He sent the enclosed check to me. You can endorse it and deposit it. I will draw $50 out and $50 the middle of the month. I am sorry there was a delay. I have $100 of Father's that I want to get back as soon as I can, but no other money here.

I had a fine drive with Dr and Mrs Wilson around Arena this afternoon. We went up 8th st to the canal, then around the Point of Rocks, Chase Drive, Eureka and Hermosa. The Wilsons were delighted. The Doctor is talking about an investment here. He intimated that he would carry some property for me if I would help pick it out and help direct it afterwards. I would like to get 10 acres this way. I am going to see if he means it. We ought to have a grove when we get older and need it. If I could raise 1/3 the value of a grove I could buy one. Maybe Ramsey[11] would finance one for us. I am going to be the Wilsons guest again tomorrow night. I wish you were here, honey. It is selfish to have these good things alone. I wanted you there this afternoon. It was a beautiful day and you would have enjoyed it.

I will see about sending the Press to you tomorrow. I am going to send you a box of oranges in a couple of weeks from Brown. I am sending one to the Sec'y, Galloway,[12] Taylor, and Father from Chase. I wish you and the boys were here tonight. Give them each a love and a kiss. With much love to you.

Affectionately, Harold

Pomeroy is coming to see me tomorrow. He is begging like a child to be kept. He said it would kill his Father and Mother. He went the limit with the widow. She is a bad one. I would not condemn him for that as he is inexperienced, and he is not safe in our work. Taylor has put it up to me to decide. My decision now is to send him east and give him till July 1st to get another place and have White[13] come here. Mrs Taylor and Mrs Stuby say to give him another chance, but I don't feel that his head is level enough to be safe in our work. This is the reason why I have decided. What do you think? Am I unjust to him? I don't see that I am. Neither does Stuby.

GLENWOOD MISSION INN

Sunday March 7

My dearest Gertrude: I am anxious to hear how much of a storm you had in Washington and whether it blew you down in the Park. I imagine it must have been pretty severe. I hope the water has not been in the cellar. I am glad to hear that you will have a new heater installed. Don't pay for it until everything is satisfactory. I have wondered how the bulbs and shrubs look. I would leave in a minute if I could. To be at the Glenwood is all right if you can have your family, but such elegance loses its best charm when you are separated from those you love the most. Our work here is in fine shape and is more highly regarded than ever. Stuby, McKay and I go to Coronado tomorrow morning. Last night I took dinner with the Wilsons. They can't get over the pleasure of meeting me here, and the satisfaction in our work, they feel as though I was one of their family. Dr says he has never known anyone in public life who had more universal support and who has enterered more into the life of the people. He says the Riversiders feel a proprietary ownership in all that we do. Likewise they said I was the best dancer that has been at the Glenwood this winter. There was a dance last night and I took a few whirls. It was too hot so I only danced half a dozen times.

Tonight I take dinner with Mr and Mrs McDuffy and Miss McDuffy. Tomorrow I have dinner again with the Wilsons at Coronado. The 16th Mr and Mrs Irving give a dinner here in my honor and have invited about 70. Mrs Loring[14] said to tell you she was sorry you could not be here. The Wilsons sent their love to you. They left this morning. They want to meet you and the boys. Anne is the best liked girl here. She is about 22, vivacious, full of fun and always with dignity. She and I danced a barn dance last night and we got bouquets from every side. It is lots of fun if you enter into it and let your self out.

I am going over to Mr Chase's now for an hour. Kiss the boys. With a great deal of love to all of you.

Affectionately, Harold

Sunday, Mar 7
Look at the editorial on the Sec'y in last nights Press. I managed to have it sent.[15] Cut out everything about our work.

━━━━━━

HOTEL DEL CORONADO

March 11 [1909]

Dearest Gertrude: I have been so rushed for several days there has not been time for writing. Thursday Mr Boal[16] the manager of a big Boston corporation took us all over the country near here. Monday night I had dinner with the Wilsons. They left Tuesday morning. Yesterday a Mr. Allen,[17] who I have known since I came to California took us as far inland as Lakeside. We stopped at La Mesa, Lemon Grove, Spring Valley and several other places. At Lakeside I met Mr Perkins of Newark, New York, the nurseryman who bought Mr Chase's interest in the Chase Bros Nursery when he came to California. We came back over a most picturesque route, the Mission Canyon road, by the San Diego Mission and then into town. We rode about 60 miles. Last night I was the guest of the McDuffee family. They left this morning. Today I have had a busy one. I have always wanted to know about the lemon oil and other by product business. There is one factory at National City but they have been so secretive, no one knows anything about their business. The plant has recently been bought by a Mr Richards[18] who owns the beautiful large brick residence on the ocean front. Do you remember it? It is the finest place here. I got an introduction yesterday and had an appointment today. He took me to the factory, showed me everything and is anxious to cooperate with us in every way. It rained hard and we went down in his big auto. We had dinner at the club in San Diego. When he found out I was related to the Gardiners he took me through his house and had me meet his family. It is a regular museum of animal heads, baskets, curios, etc. Richards is a widely known man. He is very wealthy and is one of the men who was caught in the tangle of the western land frauds. He has been indicted by a grand jury but is out on a writ of error and will be tried again. He will turn over his factory to us for experimental work.

I am going back to Riverside tomorrow and will finish writing my lemon bulletin. It will take two or three days.

Here is an interesting series of circumstances for you. I made a great impression on the McDuffee family. Mr McDuffee is one of the largest crockery manufacturers in America and a business man of the highest standing. He is a Scotchman. I noticed from the first that he looked me up every evening at the Glenwood and he invited me to dinner two or three times, but I did not accept until Sunday night. Mrs McDuffee and her daughter Mrs Never I met last winter and she (Mrs) met me like a long lost friend when I came back. I did not even remember her and only recalled her mother after some hard thinking. They were very friendly with the Wilsons and praised me to the skies every day. I had been disturbed by their courtesies and it occured to me that they might think I was single and that they were doing it for their daughter who is a woman about our age and very attractive. Then I thought it was a personal conceit and dropped it, but after a day or two I spoke to Mrs Wilson and asked her if she thought the McDuffees were trying to palm their daughter off. In the meantime, I brought in as quickly as it occured to me that I was much married. I thought of course they knew it. Well it flashed over all the Wilsons at once that I guessed right and that explains the high valuation of my stock. Sure enough the next day Mr McDuffee said he was delighted to find that I was a family man, that I must be a wonderful husband and father and that my face showed generations of good breeding. The old gentleman has been game to the last. If he was disappointed he took it out by showing more attention than ever. I am sorry if the daughter had any misapprehension about my eligibility as it never occured to me that they didn't know. Such are the incidents of travel. The Wilsons have had a good deal of fun over it.

The drive yesterday was a beautiful one. The country is carpeted with green and the series of rounded hills looked as though they had been mowed with a lawn mower. I suppose sheep had eaten everything last fall. We had a good car. The trip through the Canyon, about 5 miles, was one of the most picturesque I have ever taken. I wished for you many times. You would have enjoyed it to the full. It is too bad that so many trips come to me that you can't have with me. I never feel right about it. If you had been an heiress with an income of $50,000 we might have done a lot of traveling.

I miss you and the boys very much. If I had more time on my hands I would be lonesome, but I have not had a chance for that. I think I am gaining flesh. I have had a bad catarrah since I came. Dr Wilson gave me something to spray. It has been pretty bad, but I think is getting better. Tell the boys to write me letters. I want to hear about their school and what they do, and the flowers. Stuby and Mac are here for supper, so I will stop. Kiss and hug the boys for me.

I have a seal ring which I found in Los Angeles Friday. It fits my little finger. I have had a P. carved on it. It has the word "Mizpah" in it, 14 carat. It was in the station. I am going to get one something like it for you before I come back.

With much love,
Affectionately, Harold

What does Mizpah mean?[19]

78

March 12

My dearest Gertrude: I got back here tonight and was glad to get your letter of the 5th. I will be glad to see all of the new dresses. You will have to wear a different one every night to show them. I hope the salary check reached you before you were entirely out of money. I asked Taylor again to send them direct to you so I think you will get them all right from now on.

Stuby and I came up to Los Angeles this morning. Lyman Brown was on the train from Los Angeles. I am going to his house to dinner again Sunday. He is trying to organize a big company and wants me in it.

Woodford also went at me this afternoon to know if *I would come into the Exchange.* They want an associated manager to handle the problems arising between the associations and the Los Angeles office.[20] He would be in the country and half of each week. He said he could arrange a contract over a term of years that would be satisfactory to me. He said I could practically name my terms. I am going to look into it and see what it is. He said he wanted me in line to take his place. I imagine they would make a contract for 3 years for $20000 to $25000. I don't quite like the line of work but if I wanted to change it would make it possible for us to own a place out here in a few years. We could live on $3500 to $4000 and save the rest for investment. What do you think?

I had a wire from Taylor today saying that Shamel[21] had left today and would be here Tuesday. He has a form of nervous prostration and will probably be with us during the spring.

I am sorry the wrong picture was sent to Harold. The right one was rolled up in paper in the desk drawer. I told Taylor it was in paper.

I am afraid if Marian comes you may have more whooping cough. I am sorry they have it.

I miss you, my dearest, and wish you were here. I give you more than a hug if you were. Kiss the boys for me. With much love
Affectionately Harold

My dearest Gertrude: This has been a busy day. John Burroughs is spending the day here. I met him yesterday and he asked at once if I was George's son. He knows Father. He is a distinguished guest. The university professors are here in train and hold meetings tomorrow.[22] Wheeler will be here. This noon they were asked to a lunch in honor of Mr Burroughs and Mrs Richardson asked me to preside. I made a short address which Mr Burroughs was good enough to say he appreciated and that he wished he could speak as easily as I do. The Loring dinner is to be quite an affair. The Burtons, Von Zwallenbergs,[23] the Lows,[24] Reynalds,[25] some of the Chases and about 25 altogether are coming to bow at my feet. You belong at my side, my dear and ought to be there. I will think of you. After dinner I am to speak to the guests in the parlor.

Jeffrey[26] is here today and he says that Wheeler has said that he would like to see me at the head of the Agricultural college at Berkeley. He made a mistake in Wickson.[27] From what Jeffrey said a good many have been talking about me for the place this spring. The university can't get legislative support and I could bring it all the organizations. I would rather have that than a commercial place, wouldn't you? I'll see what develops. Wheeler is expected here tomorrow. Nothing will develop now, but I may be able to see how the land lies. Jeffrey asked me if I would take it and I told him I would look into it carefully. $6000 no less.

Our work is starting well. Lots of love to the boys. I must write to Mother.

Affectionately your husband Harold

Dearest Gertrude: Yours of the 10th came a short time ago. I will draw out only 25 the middle of the month instead of $50. I drew 50 the 1st. I am sorry it has left you short. It will take me about 150 a month out here and if are too short I will try to get some of Father for a little longer time. I will send another expense account tomorrow or the next day of about $75. Send this to Father and the rest of the $150 can go on the next account.

The Eustace[28] check is for 100 and the interest on it not on the whole 4500. This had better go not later than the 15th of April. The 1st is better if there is enough. If you can't send it I will see about getting that amount and will keep it till all the accounts are in.

I should like to see the pretty dresses. I will get my suit sometime later to match your gowns. It will be fine to have the evening cloak.

John Muir has just come in. I had a fine talk with Burroughs this morning and got him a dozen Chase oranges. I will have a box start for you in a car tomorrow. I will be 2 weeks or more. I have had boxes sent to Taylor, Galloway, Wilson, Father and Dr and Mrs Wilson. So I will hold up a short time. I will send a box to Harold[29] and one to your Father. I hope your head is better. When we live in Berkeley it will be all right.

I must stop. With love to you and the boys.

Affectionately, Harold

I had dinner with Mr and Mrs Graham of the S.P. in their car last night.

GLENWOOD MISSION INN
Before breakfast Thursday
[undated, envelope postmarked March 18]

My dearest Gertrude: I enclose a note on the Loring dinner. Please save it for the scrapbook. It was a fine thing. The table was beautifully decorated and everything went off like clockwork.[30] Mrs Loring is a very experienced woman and makes a charming hostess. She said that they always considered me one of the most distinguished guests who came to Riverside and they felt honored in having the opportunity of having the guests meet me. Nice leg pull, eh? I'm in for more just like them. They can't come too fast. Mr and Mrs Reynolds have invited me to their house next week. Harry Chase has one and Lyman Brown has been after me again. I just dodge them daily. I can't help being a hot pumpkin.

Day before yesterday some of the rich cousins autoed over from Pasadena to see me. They had the chance of observing the Loring dinner. They are Frank and Fannie Harder, Laura and Will, the former a Vassar, the latter a Yaleite. Yesterday I went with them around the Chase drive, Eureka, Hermosa, Redlands, Sunset Drive, lunch at Casa Loma, then to San Bernardino. From there I took the train home and they went on to Pasadena. They had the day of their lives, they said. They are from Philmont and are Mother's cousins. They are fine people. The Wilsons had pumped them full of my usefulness. They want me to come to dinner, so do the Wilsons and so do the McDuffee's.

I am looking for Shamel today. He will be with us during the spring. I am going to Santa Barbara next week. Your letter of the 11th came lst night. Poor little Tommy.[31] I miss him too just as he misses me. I'd like to have him in my arms now and all the rest of you at once, Marian, Margaret, whooping cough and all. I am afraid you will all have whooping cough again. Did you ask the doctor about it?

I won't draw any check I don't let you know about. There isn't anything to draw. I have drawn 50, the 1st and the 25th, the 16th and will have to draw 50 again the 1st of April.

I had a note from the Sec'y. I wrote him when he was appointed. He said he learned from Mr Taft that the Southern California people acted very effectively and they contributed to his reappointment.

I am working on a plan to organize all the Cold Storage work and Transportation work of the Dep't under one management. If it works through it will be a big thing—a good deal larger than the things we have done here. The longer I think of the Exchange proposition the less it impresses me. It would be for money primarily. I think I love my work and need to do that more than money.

Love to all. Everyone at the dinner expressed regret that you were not there. None as much as I.

Affectionately, Harold

Elmon Benton brought two books for the boys yesterday. One for George Moo-cow tales and one for Clark Dog tales. Have both write me.

Riverside
Sunday pm

My dearest Gertrude: Now for a letter for you. I didn't get up very early this morning. I have been waking pretty early lately and was tired so I lay in bed a while. At nine o'clock Shamel, Dennis,[32] Fernald,[33] a Hollander who was sent here by the Sec'y, a fine young chap and I climbed Rubidoux.[34] My, but it was lovely! It was rather cloudy, thunder caps, but the air was fine. I led the bunch and had them with their mufflers wide open before we reached the top. I felt fine. It is a joy to drink in this air and to feel it go down in your lungs. I have a bully color since I came, have gained 6 pounds and though I am going harder than any other year, the change has been good for me. All of the boys marvel at my physical energy. Shamel says 'It does me good, Powell, just to see you breathe.' I must be a healthy looking bunch for everyone says 'There is no need asking you how you feel.' My nerves are getting straightened out slowly. I spoke two hours and a half straight yesterday at the Chamber of Commerce in Los Angeles to 200 people. It was as fine an audience as I ever addressed. Lawyers, doctors, merchants, 2 federal judges and every prominent lemon man in the state. I spoke an hour from the Italian slides and then the questions were fired at me for 1 1/2 hours. Judge Call came to me after it was over and said, 'Powell you could be U.S. Senator in 10 years from California, if you wanted to be.' Then Woodford took me off and sailed head first into the Exchange matter. He says he will never take no for an answer, that we can make it the greatest organization in the world, working as a team, that I have the confidence of more people than any one in the state and a lot more taffy. It don't affect my head. He says money is no object. They want me. I told him I couldn't say definitely now. There are some might alluring things about it. We could lay away 8 to $10000 in 3 years and live well. I would be away about 3 days in a week, as the position would be Field Manager of the Exchange and I would handle all the Field questions. Sometimes I think we can't afford not to accept it. Even if I wanted to go back to scientific work I could do it easily after 3 years and could save enough to educate all the boys, or to buy a home and have it clear. I imagine though we would invest all we could spare in orange or lemon groves. We don't have enough money now to feel free to enjoy lots of things we ought to. The trouble out here would be I know so many

83

fine people it would cost us more to live than in Washington. What do you think?

I would rather build up Berkeley, but I don't think the opportunity will come. If I thought it would I'd wait for it, provided there was a chance to fire the faculty and to change the financial policy. It would mean a revolution at Berkeley and I have had enough experience in administering educational work to warrant the Board in running such a risk. I am not blind to their side. I couldn't afford to risk it myself under any other conditions, as it would fail. I'd bring Weber,[35] Josh, Shamel, Tenney[36] and such men here, but it would double the salary cost and Wheeler would throw a hundred fits if that were made fundamental. He isn't ripe yet.

Woods[37] will meet me at Phoenix on the 7th. We will spend a couple of days there, then to Yuma and Imperial, then a week or more here in the orange belt, then north. I will give him the trip of his life. Harry Chase and John Burns the Passenger agent of the Santa Fe will go to Phoenix with me and make the trip.

Chase[38] of the Bureau of Chemistry is coming about the time Woods goes and 15 men from Florida, May 1st. So I don't see how I can leave for the north before May 10th to 15th. I am going to Washington and Oregon on the way home, so it will be along towards the last of May before I get home. Then I'm going to cut Europe and China out and get acquainted over again. I'll have to be in New York several days shortly after returning but that's all I see in sight. I am going to write 3 bulletins this summer, one on cold storage for Geneva, one on cooperation in Fruit Handling with Taylor, and a Farmer's Bulletin on the orange industry, and maybe a Yearbook article on "the Influence of Handling Methods on the Value of Food Products", so I have enough for 8 months steady work.

Lyman called me up for dinner today but I didn't care to go. I am tired of it. It is work now to go out and talk all the time. I want to be let alone once in a while so as to reflect and build up the weak spots in my character. Heaven knows, it needs it enough. I came up from Los Angeles with Mrs. Harry Chase yesterday afternoon. She said she was a nervous and physical wreck for years after John was born and for a year didn't average 3 hours sleep. She said she has to take dope now every once in a while, that she never sleeps a wink if she gets excited. She told me about her shopping, her new hats, stockings,

84

shirts, and got quite confidential. She is an unresponsive person, but I guess that is a mask and not an intention. She said the old people have a pretty lonely career. Frank is east now.

Your letter of Tuesday just came. I hope the Gas Heater is alright. It is the one put in first? If it isn't entirely satisfactory we ought not to keep it.

Pomeroy is in Washington. We gave him till July 1st to look up a job. I should like to see the yard now. The things must be coming through. I'll try to get some asters from Burns when I come back if the ones you start don't do well. Don't depend on Burns though. The more I think of the general cold storage and food handling scheme the better it grows. If Miss Pennington[39] would agree, the plan would go through. She is bound to make great progress in her work alone and will built a reputation. She may not feel like coming in. I could help her make one twice as big by organizing all of it on a larger scale. Wiley[40] thanked me for my help in Chicago and said he would appreciate more help there on my return if I could spare a day. He thinks I am alright.

I got my suit yesterday. It is a fine one. My dinner coat though is a wall paper affair. I've got to get another next winter.

I sent Harold a box of oranges a few days ago, also Mabel. I will send your father one this week. I must close now with love to all.

Affectionately, Harold

GLENWOOD MISSION INN

March 21

My dearest Gertrude: It has been raining most all day. Shamel came Thursday. We started to climb Rubidoux this morning but it began to rain when we were halfway up. We went to see Mr Chase and stayed to dinner. Mrs Chase asked especially to send her love to you. She is a great admirer of you, honey. She says there ought to be more like you to which I say Amen! We stayed till three o'clock and then came back in the rain.

Shamel is in pretty good shape. He is nervous and lost his nerve so that he dislikes to meet people and he forgets easily. His train of thought often stops and he can't think straight. I am going to put him in charge of Prenda[41] and Mr Reed's house. He is a lovely fellow, sympathetic, appreciative and enthusiastic. He can't tell me often enough how he appreciates my wanting to have him come. It will be a fine thing for him and he will be all right in a month or two. He thinks we have the best organization in the Bureau. I took him to Los Angeles yesterday and he saw me meet various railroad men and fruit men. He says he wouldn't miss the training for anything. I'd like to have such a man in our work. He is better than any man we have.

Woodford spent a couple of hours with me Friday night outlining the future of the Exchange if I should come in. He is anxious to have me work shoulder to shoulder with him and have definite authority over a good deal of the work. He wants me to succeed him. If one wanted straight answers and hard work it is a fine chance but I don't get excited over it.

Stuby is coming up tonight and Hosford tomorrow to see me and I have a group of Tulare Co. men coming tomorrow and a banquet in the evening for Mr Thompson, a St Paul or Minneapolis magazine owner and newspaper publisher.[42] He is an associate of big men in all walks of life. I'll show him the real kind.

I bought a suit yesterday in Los Angeles. My old suit is beginning to look grimy. I enclose a sample. It is a beautiful piece of cloth — $45. I never had such a good suit or as fine a fit as the suit I got last year. I need a new dinner coat. Mine is 2 sizes too small. It don't meet within 4 inches. I can't get one this winter. It costs an awful lot just to live and keep clothes on. I hope to get a little more next year. $250 advance. I ought to have 4000. The limit is $3500 and I've got two advances to make to get that.

I am glad Marian and Margaret are with you. Keep them as long as you can. Give them my love and give the boys each a hug and a kiss. Lots of love to you.

Affectionately, Harold

March 23d

My dearest Gertrude: The work is rolling up every day now. I am looking for Woods a little later and for Chase of the Bureau of Chemistry and for one of Swingle's men.[43] We have never been so busy as this spring. Yesterday I had a group of Tulare Co. men here, and Stuby and Hosford[44] came up from Pasadena for a conference. Last night I was one of 25 at a Banquet by the Chamber of Commerce in honor of George Thompson, Editor of the St Paul Despatch. It was good — the eating — but the speeches were punk. I am going to Los Angeles tomorrow and will try to take dinner with the Wilsons at Pasadena. Thursday night, the Reynolds give me a dinner; bows and a bunch of Magnolia ites.[45] Let them come. Tonight I go to Harry Chase's to dinner. Can't bring them along too fast.

Don't send the money to Josh. Let me know how much you can spare after the bills are paid on the first and you retain what you need. Let the grocery bill go to the 14th again. It takes 150 a month to run me here. I will use the money that would go to Josh instead of borrowing and will pay him when my last expense account comes in.

I'll not lose your ring. I have them both. Mizpah must have been a tender sentiment between two souls. Sorry they lost it, but I will think of it as a bond between us and given me by you. I will get the diamond and will look up the jade. I will get one for your 2d finger. My Mizpah is the same size as your ring and that fits your 2nd.

The heiress asked me to come to Hollywood. I replied that I was swamped, that I wanted her money, but with a wife and three boys there was nothing doing, so let's call it off. Maybe she laughed and maybe she rushed to the cyanide bottle. There is no guessing what a female will do. I had a nice note from John Burroughs this morning asking me to come to see him at Pasadena.

The sample of your waist was very pretty. We will be stunners when we walk out with my new suit and your princess gowns. Where is the waist line, under the arms or around the neck? Is it the box effect or the anatomical?

Pomeroy is in Washington and has till July 1st to get another place. I am looking for Dennis and White today.

My best salaams to Marian. Give the whole bunch, children of all sexes and grown people too a hug and a kiss apiece. Tell Clark I was glad to get his letter and will write soon.

Affectionately, Harold

––––––

Dearest Gertrude: It has been raining more than half the time since Sunday. Tuesday it was cold and the snow came down 3/4ths of the way on the mountains. I went to Los Angeles Wednesday morning and the view of the mountains was one of the finest I have ever seen. The sun was on them. I wished that you were with me. It seems a shame to be here alone.

I spoke 5 minutes to the Exchange directors and asked for $1500 worth of fruit for our storage expts. I hadn't more than taken my seat before it was passed with the remarks that 'Mr Powell can have anything he wants.' Then Mr Story,[46] the President got up and said he had learned from a member of the Ways and Means com. that I had done more by the data I submitted to secure the raise in tariff than all the rest put together. They all stood on their hind legs then and resoluted bouquets. This is funny after the way some of them went after me earlier in the session. We never stood as high as this year.

I have to speak at the L.A. Chamber of Commerce tomorrow to the Lemon Mens Club on the Sicily lemon business. I am going down tonight as the talk is at 10 o'clock.

I had dinner with the Wilsons at Pasadena Wednesday night. They take a family interest in my work. Doctor says not to go into the Exchange as I have anything I want before me in my line. If I could only be home it would be all right. I shall make no decision now. I would rather have the Berkeley place, wouldn't you? But there is no chance. I don't think Wheeler likes me. At least I never feel so when I am with him. I am certain that I don't get excited over him.

I have a big scheme I am working out, to organize all the cold storage, transportation and food handling work of the dept under my direction. This would take in the present work in Animal Industry,

Chemistry and Plant Industry. I would handle all the general policies and would develop a field force for meats, poultry, eggs, like our own. Miss Pennington could develop the technical laboratory investigations. With the present interest in all sorts of Food work this could be made one of the great pieces of investigation in the country. I haven't submitted the plan yet to anyone and won't till I have the details. If Galloway thinks it OK, then I will bring Miss P. into line and she can handle Wiley. If he approves, Animal Industry would be forced in. I can bring to bear on such work the railroads, the warehouseman and interests all over the country and could develop a campaign that would have an influence on the building up of all kinds of Food Methods. What do you think of it?

I was at the Reynolds dinner last night. The Lows and the Frazers[47] were there and all regreted your absence. Kind of punk, it was, not much romance in that bunch.

I made quite an impression on Mrs Low and I guess it means another dinner.

I am going to Prenda now with Shamel. Dennis and White and his mother came Monday. They are all at the Handy's. The car arrived yesterday and seems to be all right.[48] It will create a big interest here.

I am going to meet Woods in Phoenix the 7th. I will be with him a couple of weeks. We will go over the Salt River and Yuma projects and the Imperial Valley and then through the citrus belt and on north.

I must stop now. I will have to draw $100 the 1st. $50 of this will be part of the money for Eustace. Let some of the bills go if you have to. So far I am keeping even. I was figuring up last night and have spent just $5.00 of personal money since coming out. I am making the dinners I have out pay my bills. It is the only way I can keep even. My suit will be ready Saturday. I tried it on Wednesday. It is a fine one and will wear like iron.

Give the boys my love. I will try to write them soon. Love to Marian and Margaret and lots to you, my dear.

Affectionately, Harold

Riverside.
[envelope postmarked April 1]

My dearest Gertrude: I have been on a high jump since Sunday. Los Angeles, Pasadena, Azusa, etc. Took dinner with the Hosfords and they sent their love to you. This is just a note.

I am dwelling with the notorious now. Yesterday I took Vice Pres. and Mrs Fairbanks[49] all over Riverside in a Glenwood car and this morning I take them on Rubidoux. He knew all about my work first from [the] Secretary and there and here. He and his son have 200 acres near Redlands and he said he had heard of the wonderful results in every place he had been. We went to packing houses, inspected machinery, clipper cuts, etc. I am going to spend a day with the son and his wife later. They are here with them, also Mrs Timmons and daughter.

I took dinner with them last night and was marked as "the Friend of the Vice President." The fame of this work is spreading all over. I had all the boys come in to meet him last night.

Tomorrow I go on a 2-day trip with Woodford, Call[50] and Charters.[51]

Must stop with love to you and all.

Affectionately, Harold

———

Glenwood Mission Inn

Saturday evening 8 o'clock
April 4

My dearest Gertrude: I haven't had time for much writing this week. Things have been on one grand rush. I came home this evening from a two days auto trip with Woodford, Charters and Call. We took in every packing house in Riverside, San Bernardino and upper Los Angeles counties. I enjoyed the trip and was about done up with a grippy cold. Thursday night I was at dinner at Harry Chase's and had a fever most all night. Slept about 3 hours and rode all day yesterday. I feel better tonight. The pace out here is a strenuous affair. Lyman called me up again tonight and asked me to come to dinner tomorrow

90

but I didn't accept. It is too hard work to have to talk all this time. I am going to rest a little tomorrow. One of Swingle's men just came tonight and I will have to start him up Monday and the car will be ready to start up then. I leave for Phoenix Tuesday and will probably be with Woods till the 23d. Chase of Chemistry reaches here the 24th and there will be a crowd of Florida people here about the 1st. I will leave for the north about the 10th of May.

Miss Pennington may be here three or four days about the time Chase is. She wrote a few days ago that she wanted to see our field methods, buying, cooperation, railroad handling etc. before she started on the chicken work and that she and Dr Wiley had discussed the advisability of studying all of our methods out here. She will send a wire in a few days if she comes. I need about three more existences to keep all of these things going.

Woodford and Call were at me a dozen times about coming here. They would pay me almost anything if I would come. They want me to be Field Manager, i.e. in charge of all of the packing houses. The picking, packing, grading and everything. I would be away about ½ the week and in Los Angeles ½. They will buy me the best auto-mobile and give me anything I want. There are some mighty attrac-tive things about it and I wont turn it down until after I find out just how far they will go. I almost think they would pay me $10000. If they would, we couldn't afford not to go for 3 years. I wouldn't make a contract for less than that. I could go back to scientific work then and have several thousand ahead.

I would rather have the Berkeley place at $6000 but I don't see any chance for that. Read the editorial in tonight's Press Apr 3 on "The Citrus Experiment Station". The Berkeley people will think I wrote it. Please save it. The Berkeley people have handed them a lemon in the station. It's no good. I think Mr Reed wrote the editorial. If they don't look out the Exchange, the League and the other organizations will turn on the Berkeley people and make things warm for them. Mr Reed wants us to start a Department station here.

I enjoy your letters and all the details about the boys and the house. I miss all of you very much and wish I were home. The yard must begin to look fine. You can put on the nitrate of soda now. Scatter lightly 4 or 5 pounds of it before a rain, or put it on and then use the hose to dissolve it. The water is turned off the outside faucet over the coal bin. If you had been here for a couple of days you wouldnt have needed your coat. It was hot, about 90. I have a great tan. You wouldnt know me, I'm so handsome.

Sunday morning. I had to stop here and go down stairs to meet some people. I never had so many railroad and business men come to see me as this year. There was a masquerade ball for the employees last night. There were some funny costumes. The crowd danced too. I didn't try it but twice as I was too tired.

How I would like to have Lawrence on my lap this morning. I would sing all the songs to him, [?] and all. I was glad you could see Mrs Mulford and go to the college womens reception.

I drew out $100 April 1. This makes 175 I have drawn altogether. Let me know how much more you can spare and keep enough so as not to be short. It takes over 150 a month here. My account for about $75 was held up on account of several items. That all goes to Father. I will send another today. Send Father the balance of the 150 we owe him and the rest to me. The next month will take a lot of money on account of the travel. George's essay on the property was fine. He is a great boy. So many people ask after you every day.

If I came here and had a auto you could take a good many 2-day trips with me. Wouldnt that be fine! There are lots of things about the Exchange matter that are way ahead of the Chase offer. I would be doing the same kind of work I am doing now only for a fewer number.

I must stop now. Stuby is coming to see me today. Kiss the boys. I love you all.

Affectionately, Harold

Shamel thinks I am the Wizard of the Department.

———

Glenwood Mission Inn

April 6, 1909

Dearest Gertrude: I am sorry to hear that Clark has the measles. This means that all of them will have it. I ought to be there, my dear, to help you. Have Alice every day you can.

Clark will need to be watched with unusual care. The measles are especially apt to hit the kidneys. Have Dr Watkins watch him like a hawk so that any trouble can be checked at the start.

I am enclosing John Burrows letter. Harry Chase and John Burns and I leave for Phoenix today. There will be something in the Press tonight about the car and my trip. Please cut them out.

I am getting up a reception for Woods a week from today at the Adobe. All the boys will be here for dinner at night. The Chamber of Commerce will handle the reception. I have a great trip planned for him.

One of the Regents of the University, Mr Foster,[52] a whale of a big fellow, sent me his card last night. He is here for a day. He had heard a lot of my work and wanted to see me. I thought first it might have something to do with the Berkeley place, but it was just accidental. He told me all about the troubles up there, that they made a mistake in Wickson etc. I pumped him out and saw that he as Chairman of the Board hasn't any conception of the agricultural needs and that they are doing no more than they have to, as the older departments are still weak and they want to build them up first. It is an almost hopeless job to reorganize it as there isn't enough money available and the University wouldn't support a movement for big state appropriations as it would cut in on their regular appropriations.

We will have a demonstration at the car Tuesday before Woods reception. Mr Reed took lunch with me yesterday. He had a red hot letter following Clark's editorial on the station. He wanted me to read it before it was published. Half the letter was in psalms of praise of my work. I made him leaven it and told him to write Wheeler direct. Reed wants me to have the Berkeley place but it will fizzle it if these fruit men get busy. I am holding them back but I am afraid some of them will run over. I must close now with much love to you all.

Affectionately, Harold

April 8, 1909

My dearest Gertrude: What a ride we had yesterday! About 100 miles over half through the desert. We drove over the cultivated portions of the valley on the west side of the river and then went 40 miles to the government Granite Reef dam. It was a lovely day. I am as bronzed as a copperhead this morning. I bought a duster before leaving. Without it my clothes would be ruined. I will use it all the time now.

Woods had the trip of his life. He said he never took such a drive. I will make his eyes stand out before he leaves. Today we go across the river and will be met with two machines and will drive another hundred before night. We leave at 7 for Maricopa and have to wait there till 12.09 A.M. We will be at Yuma at 6.20 A.M., go on the 8 o'clock train to Laguna Dam and spend the rest of the day driving around Yuma, leaving at 6.20 Saturday morning for Indio and at 2.00 P.M. for Riverside.

Sunday, Monday and Tuesday we will be in Riverside, Wednesday in Redlands, Thursday and Friday en route to Los Angeles and in the city. Friday in San Diego county, Sunday at Coronado, Monday at Santa Paula, Tuesday Berkeley and Wednesday at Sacramento. Then I hike for Los Angeles, meet Chase and begin over.

Mr Chase and Harry are with us and they are having a fine trip. I hope the boys are getting on alright. Love to you all.

Affectionately, Harold

Riverside
[postmarked April 12]

My dearest Gertrude: I hope you wont get the measles. The boys will probably all have them. If you need help get a nurse for a while. I ought to be home and am sorry I am not there to help.

Busy. I have never had such a strenuous winter. Things are picking up every day. Mills takes us for a trip over the heights today. This afternoon there is a reception by the Chamber of Commerce and a demonstration of the car. Tonight I preside at a Y.M.C.A. meeting where Chapman talks and also Woods.

Next Mr Chase comes and the following week 40 Florida people. The papers are all saying that they come through my invitation. There is a lot of sectional jealousy and they are unloading the responsibility for coming on me. I can carry it. I will have to be with them several days. Miss Pennington comes the 27th the same time they are here. She will be here four or five days. She will have to go with the party on with Stuby. She couldn't come at any other time. Yesterday there were a lot of railroad people here to see the car.

I cant write more now. Kiss the boys but dont catch the measles. Mabel writes that Father bought the Russell place for $2600. That's a snap. There are 60 acres of apple land worth $100 an acre. Now he can raise the grain for the horses. The saving on that item alone will pay the interest on the place.

Lots of love.

Affectionately, Harold

THE ANGELUS, LOS ANGELES

[postmarked April 13, Riverside]

My dearest Gertrude: We had a fine trip. We rode 175 miles in two days in the desert in the Phoenix valley. Then we had a fine day at Yuma. The engineer in charge of the Reclamation works, Mr Sallon, went to Laguna Dam with us, 15 miles up the Colorado from Yuma. This dam is a mile wide. We drove back in the thickest dust I ever saw. We had a 4-mule team. We stayed at the barracks[53] at Yuma and I slept on a cot out of doors till 2.45 A.M. when we left yesterday for home. It was a delightful experience, pretty strenuous but worth while. We either got off or took the train three mornings at 2 or 3 o'clock. Yesterday afternoon Harry took Woods all over town in the auto and this morning Lyman took us with Shamel and Fernald over the Highgrove district, then to Colton back through West Riverside, then down to that tract towards Los Angeles and home — 45 miles. It was a fine drive and I wished for you and the boys. Tomorrow morning Mr Rumsey takes us over his groves. In the afternoon Frazer takes us on the Heights. The next morning we look through the packing houses, in the afternoon we have a demonstration at the precooling car and a reception afterwards by the Chamber of Commerce. Wednesday Lyons takes us over Redlands. Thursday Lyman, Harry, Shamel and I start for Los Angeles and visit packing houses. At night we go to San Diego by sleeper, tour over San Diego Friday and back to Los Angeles by sleeper and return to Riverside in Lyman's auto by way of Orange county. I shall try to get Woodford to go to San Diego with us.

Shamel is getting on finely. He has improved a great deal since he came and will be alright again in a couple of months. Later: the boys all came over and we walked on Rubidoux. We had a big scare. I led the crowd and at one place I ran down one hill and up another. This was on top. Woods followed me on a run and it was too much for him. He fell and lost consciousness. We fanned him and rubbed him for a while and then I ran for an auto at the top to take him down, but he came out by the time I got back and we walked slowly down. It might have been a serious thing. I will not do any more running. I did last Sunday and we all puffed like engines. It is not as easy or safe to do this as it was when we were 20. Woods has been confined for a couple of years to the office and is pretty tired. He has begun to realize what our work is. He had no conception of it before and he is enthusiastic over it. He is having the trip of his life.

You can send the expense account to Father, $59.50. The remainder $15.60 will be in the next account. It was an error of mine in dating the receipts. I am anxious to know how much there is in the bank. I will draw $75 on the 15th. I am broke now and have borrowed $20 of White. Send the balance of the 150 to Father when the next expense account comes in and send me a check for the balance and all you can spare. I will get $100 if we are too low. It ties up $150 to $200 to keep me going out here and I dont want you to be short. When I get 8000 from the Exchange we wont be so short.

I am glad Clark hasn't the measles. His kidneys will need to be watched very closely when he does have them. Tell him his report was fine. George will have to hustle and have a better one. Kiss them all. With much love to you

Affectionately, Harold

[postmark Riverside April 17]

My dearest Gertrude: We had a great trip in San Diego Co. yesterday, two machines and 95 miles. Woods is having the trip of his life. We came up on a sleeper last night and start in a few minutes for Whittier, Fullerton, Orange and Riverside in Lyman's car. Tomorrow we have dinner with Mr Chase.

Woodford came at me again night before last about coming here. There is no trouble in getting $25000 on 3 years contract, and I think 500 for expenses of moving out. I am going to talk with him definitely before I leave. We would live in Los Angeles and I would be home 4 nights a week and Sundays. I am almost afraid we cant afford not to take it. If I wanted to be Secretary it could be done easier from here than anywhere else. Woods dont want me to decide before coming to Washington. But of course the very best they can do there in salary is 3500. It is fixed by law. Woods has just begun to realize the hold we have out here.

I am looking for Miss Pennington Thursday and the Florida bunch and Chase about the same time. I will be busy till I leave. I want to start north as early as possible next month. I am anxious to get home and to see you all. I hope the boys are getting on alright. I think of you every few minutes and wish I was there to help you. Love to the boys and to you.

Affectionately, Harold

Hotel Hayward, Los Angeles

April 19

My dearest Gertrude: We have begun another busy week. We came down this morning. Mr Chase was on the train with us. All of the Chases are much pleased with Wood and Shamel. We were there yesterday for dinner. Today we have met the railroad people and Woods looked over the Exchange very carefully. Tomorrow we go to Santa Paula and on to Santa Barbara at night. Wednesday we will be at Santa Barbara and Woods and Stuby go north at night and I return to Los Angeles Thursday. Chase and Miss Pennington come Friday.

The Chases have asked me to bring them there Sunday to dinner with Shamel. Shamel is a new man. He has gained 20 pounds and his nerves are in much better shape.

Wednesday morning. The Potter.[54] Santa Barbara. I am overlooking the ocean and a beautiful lawn and banks of flowers from my window. I did not have a chance to finish at the Hayward. We had the finest inland ride yesterday I ever took. Teague[55] brought us from Santa Paula in a big touring Franklin. We came through the mountain canyons for 15 miles. The road a good share of the way was under live oaks and the mountains on both sides are heavily covered with low growing shrubbery and grass. The shrubs were in full bloom and so were thousands of flowers. The only other drive I ever took that approaches it is the Amalfi drive. That is next to the sea. The road is cut out of the mountain side a good deal of the way. It was 50 miles from Santa Paula.

I am going back with Teague tonight as far as Ventura and will take the train from there at 5.40 to Los Angeles. Teague is a splendid driver and he has a fine car. We have covered 800 miles in autos since Woods came. Today we will cover 100 miles. He never had such a trip before. He sees the meaning of our work now. Stuby and Hosford are here and ride with us to the lemon districts today. Stuby is not very well. He has some intestinal trouble. It may be appendicitis.

The Potter is the best located hotel I have seen. It is back from the ocean and back of it are the mountains.

They are waiting for me for breakfast. My letters are pretty choppy, the pace has been so fast I am way behind in all kinds of writings. I hope the boys are alright. I wish you were here. Give lots of love and kisses to the boys. With lots to you.

Affectionately, Harold

GLENWOOD MISSION INN

April 22

My dearest Gertrude: I am on a jump from place to place so fast I hardly have time to think when I write. I forgot to tell you about the checks I have drawn. On the 15th I drew one on the Hayward Hotel for

$20, on the 18th one on the Glenwood Hotel Co. for $60; and today the 22d I will have to draw one for $20. My last expense account must be in by this time so I hope I am not overdrawing. I will draw $50 again on the 1st and I may have to draw 475. I will write Father for 100 to come home on as it will take all of that extra when I go north. The expense account that should be in now ought to cover these extras. It's a corker to be so poor and not know where the next $50 is coming from. 8000 a year looks better to me, the more I contemplate its bigness.

I am going to have a talk with Woodford before I leave. Woods says he would not advise me not to take it. He told a group of men yesterday that he had been in the Dept 15 years, that he had looked over the work of a great many men but he had never seen a piece of work so completely in hand as we have ours. He says it is the best piece in the bureau. It takes half the life out of it though to be away from you and the boys so much. I don't like it. It isnt right for any of us.

I had a glorious ride yesterday back to Ventura through the mountains. They were covered to the top with wild lilac in bloom, sumac and a beautiful clematis, cream colored, ran over all and was in full flower. How I wished for you! Some day we will take it in our machine.

I have a letter from Fred Fairbanks this morning asking if I can spend a day on his ranch at Redlands. He lives in Pasadena and has a machine. I am going to suggest that he take Chase, Miss Pennington and me from Redlands to Pasadena and visit packing houses on the way. He wants especially to see them and so do they so I can kill several birds with one stone. This will be next week some day. They come some time tomorrow.

I went to Los Angeles last night and ran out here on the 7:30 train this morning. I am going back to Los Angeles this evening to fix up the Florida trip.

I am fat honey. I weigh 181. I have gained 10 lbs since coming out and considerable of it is under my vest. I had a nice letter from Hilda and one from Emma.[56] I enclose them. Did your Father get the oranges?

I must go. I have about 25 letters to dictate and came over purposely for them. Lots of love to you all.

Affectionately, Harold

April 24

My dearest Gertrude: I wish you were here. now. Miss Pennington came this morning and will probably be in the state about a week. She will join the Florida party next week. Chase comes tonight or tomorrow. He will also get on the Florida band wagon. Tomorrow we go to dinner at the Chases. This afternoon we take in the packing houses and Rubidoux in the morning. It is hot here today and is getting hotter.

I am planning now to get away. I hope to leave by the 8 or 10th and to be home by the 20th. I never want to be away so long again. You ought to see the roses here now. I have never seen them more beautiful. There has been more rain this year than in several years and the whole country is green to the tops of the hills. They are beginning now though to show a trace of brown on the tops.

This is just a note while I am waiting for dinner. I hope the boys are not having the measles and that Clark is well again. Give them all my love and kiss apiece. With much love to you.

Affectionately, Harold

April 28

My dearest Gertrude: This week is a mad rush. Monday Harry and Mrs Chase, and Lyman and Mrs Brown came to the Glenwood to dinner to meet Miss Pennington and Frank and Mrs Chase came over in the evening. During the day we were at packing houses. In the evening Mr Hill[57] the engineer in charge of the western Reclamation projects and Mr Newell[58] the Director of the Reclamation Service came from Los Angeles to see me, so we had quite a party. They are both big men and Miller gave me the Presidential suite for them at $5.00 a day. What do you think of that? Miller does everything for me. He offers me an auto any time I need one. Did I write he had changed my room three times? When the season was on I was in the annex. Then he changed me to the top of the stairs, 1st floor in the main building to one of the large rooms without bath—a regular reception room. Now I have a big room and bath on the same floor—all for 1.25 a day for my room. Yesterday Lyman and Mr Chase in his new auto took us all over both ends of Riverside to see the irrigation systems and last night we all came here. Newell says if there is anything here I dont own he would like to know about it.

Here I am with 45 Floridians on my hands. They are looking to me to guide them and show them the industry. Woodford has had to go to Washington on Tariff matters and I guess I'll have to take them in tow. Today we are at the Exchange meeting. Tomorrow in the Azusa-Glendora-Pomona district. Friday at Riverside, Saturday in Redlands. Stuby and Miss Pennington help as guides. She has caught on to all the packing house wrinkles.

Sunday the Browns have invited us to dinner. Monday I come to Los Angeles again to speak to the Florida bunch and Miss P— starts east. She has gathered a great deal from our methods that will apply to her work. She is the keenest person I ever took through the industry. Everybody here likes her. Mrs Chase fell in love with her and Mr Chase had his arm around her inside of an hour. I told her it was a dangerous thing to have such examples before me.

Woodford left hurriedly for Washington and I did not have a chance to talk with him and will probably not see him before I leave. He wrote me that he wanted me to let him bring the matter before the Board and that they could not get along without me. I am more tempted with this than I have ever been before and I am afraid we cant afford to let it go by. $8000 a year is better than $3000 and it would be the same sort of work I am doing now.

I am planning now on getting away as soon as I can after the Florida people go. It will take several days to close up things here and I will probably have to go to San Diego. I think I can get away by the 10th. I will spend a day at Berkeley and go north to Oregon and Washington. It will probably be about the 25th before I reach Washington. I am anxious to get back. It has been the most strenuous winter yet. I haven't called on the Reynolds and must do it before I leave. It means an evening or a Sunday afternoon and I haven't had the time.

Clark's letter about the baby calling everybody a skunk was very funny. I have laughed and laughed over it. He said not to bring him anything unless he stopped calling everybody a skunk. The little monkey. I am so anxious to see him. Yes I got the pictures. They are fine. I have them with me.

I must close now and go to breakfast. It is 7.30. I have been up since 6.00. I tried to write Monday and yesterday but didn't get a chance. Give my love and a kiss to each boy and tell them I will come home as soon as I can. With much love to you.

Affectionately, Harold

I imagine the expense acct is in now. I am drawing a check this morning for 425 on the Hotel Hayward.

THE GLENWOOD

April 30

My dearest Gertrude: I am going to join the Cooks Tourist bunch. Yesterday I ran the Florida outfit, covered 20 places in autos and were on time at every place. I'm it all right with them. Stuby, Chase, Pennington and Dorsey of the Soils bureau were along. They are here now and I ran them today in the Riverside district and tomorrow in Redlands. It is strenuous. Last night we had a meeting here and Mr Chase spoke to them. They are depending on me to keep them in everything.

I have been working hard since 5 A.M. I am behind with my work and haven't a minute in the day time. I got the check for 80 and destroyed it as I sent you a statement of the checks drawn. I wrote Father and asked him to send you 100 for deposit to bring me home. I will draw $75 day after tomorrow for the first.

This is just a note. I will try to write more Sunday. I am feeling well but a little tired.

Kiss the boys and here is one for you.

Affectionately, Harold

My dearest Gertrude This has been a great day for the Florida people. There were 14 autos. I handled the bunch on schedule again. This morning we went all over the Heights, and through the packing houses on that end of town, and this afternoon through the town houses and over the Chase drive and Rubidoux. They were simply overcome. The thing is so big and so picturesque, it makes them gasp.

Tomorrow we go at 7.28 to Redlands and return here at night. I shall probably shake them Monday and go to San Diego Monday night. Miss Pennington goes Tuesday. Her reputation and mine are both ruined. Nearly everyone in the Florida bunch has called her Mrs Powell. Stuby thinks its a great joke. So you want me to be Secretary of Agriculture, do you? Well, I would like to be myself but I'm not losing sleep over it. I could get it from here easier than from Washington.

I can't write more. This is a note slipped in while waiting for the . crowd for supper. Love to all.

Friday night   *Affectionately, Harold*

———

My dear Gertrude: The strenuous week ended in an automobile ride from which we emerged looking like painted minstrels. The Redlands folks took us through some packing houses there on Smiley Heights and over the Sunset drive. The luncheon was at the Casa Loma. After that a lot of autos from across the valley took the party to East Highlands and then over some dusty high drives to San Bernardino.

There was a dance here last evening. The last of the season. Mrs Green and Mrs Girdlestone were here and asked after you and the boys. Moulton has gone out of the fruit business, and is President of the First National Bank.

The Florida bunch returned to Los Angeles last night and will be there during considerable of the week. I will meet them again Wednesday. They want to organize an exchange down there. Dr. Inman and a couple of others asked me yesterday if I would consider the managership at $10000. How would you like to live in Ocochobee or Callosahatchie Florida on $10000? I wouldn't take the job for less than a million and seventeen dollars a day. Everyman in the state would think you were robbing him.

Stuby, Chace, Miss Pennington and I go to San Diego tomorrow morning to see the By Product business and our lemon work. Chace is an oyster. I'll give him a chance before I make up my mind about him but I am shaky about his ability to make good. He hasn't keen intuition and lacks the qualities that make a field man. Miss Pennington goes Wednesday to Kansas and there begins rounds of [?] to arrange for her work. She has grasped this industry quicker than any person I ever saw and has gained a lot of help for her work. If I stay in the Department the two lines will be closely associated as the machinery and the principles are the same for both. I have an idea though that I will come to California about the first of next year. I hate to think of dropping the Dept work but if I can do the same kind of work and get more than twice the salary it will be hard to turn it down.

I thought from reading Eustace's letter that he would like to come back. We will give him a place if he wants to change at any time. The bills I have drawn since the 15th are on that card. These are not in addition to the one drawn regularly on the 15th but include all of them. It is hard not to get our accounts mixed. I run out of money suddenly and have to draw some money quickly. I have kept as close account as I can of the money in the bank and have tried not to overdraw. I hope I haven't. I shall draw 475 tomorrow. This covers the May 1st fund.

The garden must look fine. I would put in a few of the gladiolis before I return — 2 every week. This will give a succession of bloom. If we should go to California I would have to paint and paper the house so as to have it look well. I think we ought to get 7000 to 7500 for it. Ashleys price of 8000 is too high.

Miss Pennington and I go to Lymans to dinner tonight. As we were leaving the Florida bunch yesterday, one of them came up and said, "I hope you and the Madame will come see us in Florida." Most of them thought she was "Mrs Powell."

Love to the boys and you.

Lovingly, Harold

May 5

My dearest Gertrude: I am waiting here for the Florida people to gather. They sent word that they wanted me to be here sure. I supposed it was for an evening meeting, and I was put wise a few minutes ago that they have collected $150 or $200 and that three of us, Burton of the Exchange who has done a great deal for them, Dr Inman of Florida who organized the party, and I are to be handed dynamite, gold canes, watches, diamonds, loving cups or some such thing as a token of their appreciation of what we have done for them. I wouldn't mind an automobile. I hate loving cups but I appreciate their kindly feelings. The southerners are great on hospitality. It seems they wanted to hold a smoker last evening and present the things then but I guess they were afraid to risk it as a member of them would surely get hilarious.

Yesterday we were at San Diego and Mr Allen took us to a lot of houses in his machine. We came back to Riverside last night. Miss Pennington left this morning for the east. She had a fine time and has a splendid idea of our field methods. After she saw me handle the Florida crowd and saw how the people looked on our work she wrote Wiley that I am a marvel in handling men and things in the field and that she never saw a man who had bouquets fired at him from every side every day and yet who paid no attention to them, but went right on with his job. If my head was affected by bouquets it would have burst long ago.

I am planning now to be home on the 22nd. I will probably leave for the North Monday or Tuesday, or if I don't go to Oregon I will take a few more days to finish up here. At any rate I am trying to reach home on Saturday the 22nd so as to have Sunday with you. I will have to be a day in Chicago on the way with the railroad men and with the cold storage people. I promised Miss Pennington to see some more people in the interest of her work and I have to see Nickerson in regard to the next International Congress.

I had a wire from Father today saying he had sent you a check for $100 to be deposited for me. Dont draw on this as I need it to finish up and to pay my expenses home.

I think I wrote that I had the baby's pictures which you sent. they are fine.

Loving cups are flying in every direction.

This morning Miss Pennington brought out a knit tie which she said was for me. She said her conscience troubled her after she and Helen promised one and then didn't do it. She said it was official. It is a beauty—blue and double. It isn't quite finished but will be sent me as soon as it is done. Now if some one will give me an extra pair of trousers I will be pretty well supplied. I need a new hat too.

I am anxious to see the garden. From what you have written I judge it is coming on finely. I will be glad to be home and hoe it and tend it myself. If we should come out here we would have a beautiful lot of flowers and plants. I would like some day to build an adobe house with pilasters on the outside and beams inside, something like Lyman Browns. I like that better than the Chases. I must close now with much love to you and the boys.

Affectionately, Harold

Later: they gave each of us a big loving cup. It is a beauty.

━━━━━

Glenwood May 7

My dearest Gertrude: I am packing things up and am beginning to count they days before I reach home. I leave here Monday, go to Berkeley from Los Angeles Wednesday night, to Sacramento Saturday and leave for Chicago about Sunday or Monday. I will be in Chicago 2 days with the railroad men, cold storage people and Miss Penningtons work. I will reach Washington the afternoon sometime of the 22nd. I haven't looked up time tables but will probably come in over the Pennsylvania. I can decide that in Chicago and will wire you. I will take dinner and spend an evening with Harold and Emma but will stay at a hotel down town as it is so much more convenient to have a room there when I am busy. I don't know just what day I will arrive but will write them a note and then will call them up after I reach there.

Today I am with Dorsey, Lyman is taking us around this morning. This is a short break while he is doing some business. We go to Highgrove at any minute. This afternoon Mr Chase takes us in his machine over the heights and to Corona. Tomorrow I am with Fred

Fairbanks, the Vice President's son at Redlands and here. Sunday I will make calls and Monday afternoon leave.

Stuby goes home for a couple of weeks. He has had an intestinal infection and thought it was tuberculosis. He was at the hospital a couple of days and had a thorough bacteriological examination made. It isn't what he feared and he feels better. But he will have to lay off a while and take local treatment.

I drew $50 on Father's $100 this morning. I will probably draw 50 more on this and 50 on salary the 15th. I am sending in an expense account of $171 today. When this comes in we will add $29 and pay Eustace the money for April and July. Our insurance and interest are due in July too. $8000 a year looks good to me. Maybe I can raise it to $10000. Woodford is in Washington on tariff matters and may be there some time. Call is there with him. I may not see him again. I wanted to have another talk with him before I left.

You ought to see the cup. It is a beautiful thing and perfectly useless. It has three horn handles and a base. One Floridian who was pretty full said it cost $75.[59] If they had given a watch or diamond ring it would have been worthwhile but a cup is only good to look at. They meant well though and I accepted it in the spirit in which it was given. One of the Glenwood boys wanted to know if I won it. I guess he thought I was in a foot race.

I must close with much love to you and the boys.

Affectionately, Harold

Glenwood Sunday morning
[postmarked May 9]

My dearest Gertrude: I had a pretty good sleep last night and am feeling a little rested but I have let down and feel heavy after the rush of the winter. I am trying to take it as easy as I can in closing up. I am going north Wednesday night and will leave Sacramento Tuesday and Chicago sometime Friday. Send letters to the Auditorium annex.

It has been a pretty strenuous winter but a more successful one than ever before. With Tenney and Pomeroy out and Stuby half sick we are short of men but the work is in good shape.

I am going to express the loving cup tomorrow. It won't go in my trunk. I sent another box of oranges from the Chases yesterday and Mr Rumsey asked for your name so that he could send you a box. We ought to have plenty of fruit to finish up the orange season.

Woodford and Call will be in Washington probably when I return. I want to have them to dinner Monday or Tuesday. You can have Alice that day to help. They are fighting for the increase in lemon tariff. I want to see Woodford again and hope he will be there. I think I will acept a place with them if we can reach a satisfactory agreement. I am not sure that I shall not make it $10000 a year. I would take $8000, but think I could raise it to 10. That would give us a chance to save $5 or $6000 a year and start buying groves. I would begin to invest in groves as fast as I had enough for a first payment. We would sell all of our beds and old furniture and start new. We would probably rent for a couple of years until we could get enough to buy a lot and build a house.

I have talked with Mr Rumsey, Chase and Reed and they think it would be a great thing for the industry if I should come here. Reed wants me to take the Berkeley place but I don't see much of a chance for that. I would like to see Woods take Berkeley. If I were in the state I could throw all the influence of the organizations that way and would work hand in hand with him. I would rather have the Exchange in some ways. It would be easier work, along the line I am most interested in and with a problem already organized.

Mr Reed has just gone. He has been with me two hours. He is a grand old man. He will probably come east this fall and I have invited him to come and stay with us in Washington. He will be there in September if he comes.

I think the plan of going to Ghent and staying at the Garners with the boys home is a fine one. I would like to take a couple of weeks there and then a couple of weeks later. I may have to go to Oregon in July—probably will have to. Gallaway wired that he would like to have me go there to look into several matters. We will have to arrange the time when I get back. We can pay all expenses by renting 2 months—July and August.

I am counting the days till I return. I wish I didn't have to stop in Chicago but I feel that I must take the time to get our work well rounded up with the railroad men.

I got a ball and knife for each Clark and George and a Chinese sword for Lawrence. Don't you wish you knew what I have for you!

I must go now. I have to call on the Chases and Brown and the Handys. I have invited Dennis and his mother here to dinner as my guests tonight.

Kiss the boys. With much love.

Affectionately, Harold

━━━━━

[written on Hotel Hayward letterhead,
Tuesday night en route to San Francisco.
Postmarked Oakland May 12]

My dearest Gertrude: I am starting back at last, thank heaven. It seems an age since I left home. I will have to spend an hour every day just getting acquainted with you and the boys. I don't like these long trips any more than you do although the constant change to new things makes it easier for me than it is for you. I hope we can get settled down pretty soon.

I left Riverside yesterday afternoon. I had dinner at the Handy's. Everyone sent love to you. Miss Fuller wasnt there to dinner but she rushed over to see me for a couple of minutes.

I had Dennis and his mother to dinner with me at the Glenwood Sunday night. Mrs Dennis appreciated it very much. She thinks I am pretty good to her James and that I am—a wizard at handling people. I took lunch with the Hosfords at Pasadena today. Shamel and White have moved down there. Shamel is very much improved. He has gained 25 pounds.

If I can make it I will go to New York from Chicago for the 20th and be home the 21st. The American committee to handle the next Refrigerating Congress will be organized and I ought to be there. Taylor wired about it yesterday. I am afraid I cant get there in time unless I cut out Chicago. That is as important as the New York end. I ought to have been twins.

I wouldn't be surprised if the Florida people made me a definite offer. Burton of the Exchange said this morning that they talked quite a little about it. I wouldn't go though. I would rather have the

California place if I made a change. They cant make an offer until after they organize in June.

I am going to bed very early tonight. I have drawn the 2d $50 on Father's deposit and on the 15th I will draw another and a final $50. Give the boys much love. With a great deal to you.

Affectionately, Harold

HOTEL ST FRANCIS, SAN FRANCISCO

May 12, 1909

My dear Gertrude: I had lunch here and will drop a line before starting out. I called on the SP people this morning and some of the Santa Fe. I have an upper berth and Mr Horsburg is trying to get me a lower. Everything is very full.

San Francisco looks like a new city. You wouldn't know there had been a quake. The buildings are fine. There is a great deal of building going on yet but the bare spaces are well filled.

I thought I could call on Mrs Mayhew but will not have time. I go to Sacramento in the morning. Today is Commencement so it is not easy to see the university folks. I left my card in Wheelers office.

Stuby is getting on slowly. He was in bed this morning. Mrs Stuby looks as strong as an ox. She seems to have a great constitution. I will be there tonight.

I think now I will be home on the 21st from New York. I can't tell what time till after I reach there. I will let you know.

I am anxious to get back. I want to see you and the boys very much. I must go now. With love to all of you.

Affectionately, Harold

[postmarked May 14]

Dearest Gertrude: I am so far along. I came over here yesterday afternoon and met a number of fruit men and had a talk with Judge Shields.[60] I am going to meet Mackie this morning and then go and see Jeffrey.

This is a dirty town compared with the Southern California places and the people are a tougher looking lot. You can see the effect of the saloon on the people on the street. Riverside for a clean, orderly livable place is way ahead of them all.

I hope you have received some of the oranges by this time. We ought to have a good supply in the next couple of weeks if all the boxes arrive. I will get a box of lemons and one of grape fruit.

I had several wires from Taylor yesterday. In one he said that Tenney had wired he couldn't go to the Florida meeting next week. I wired back that he must go and that nothing must interfere. I had a later wire saying he would go.

The Florida people hold a big convention on the 20th and I promised them to have Tenney there. The whole convention will be given over to organization and to the handling question. I think we will lose Tenney in another year. He wants to go to the farm. I would try to get Eustace back if he left. If I should leave, the work would disorganize. Stuby isn't a leader. He is too pessimistic and slow to lead anything. He would have to handle the western work but it would lack snap and imagination. It is a hard thing to find men who can see a whole problem. Tenney comes nearer a leader than any of the boys. He is an old grandfather though in a good many ways When it comes to monitoring obstacles and riding over them all, Hosford beats the boys to a finish.

I will be home on the 21st some time. I will go to New York from Chicago and will take the first train home when we get though. Kill a calf and a pig or two. You may be eaten yourself if you don't provide well. Give the boys a kiss and much love.

Affectionately, Harold

May 18, 1909

My dearest Gertrude: I got three letters from you just now, one written on the 7th, one sent to Berkeley and one here. I was glad to get them as it has been a long time since I have heard.

I am going to dinner with Emma and Harold. I called Emma this morning. She said Harold had been sick for a week and had gone to the office for the first time. He has some stomach trouble.

I had a note from Miss Pennington this morning saying that she would be at the New York meeting and that she would be in Chicago tonight or tomorrow morning. She goes on the Pennsylvania. I have my ticket on the Lake Shore. I am sorry we cant go together. She was disturbed about a letter she had sent me at the Sutter Club written from the Overland Limited. Evidently it was the wrong letter in my envelope as she asked to have it returned unopened as she sent my letter to another man and I evidently had his. I left a forwarding address, so if it comes hold it and I will return it to her.

I wish I were starting home tonight instead of to New York. I think I will leave about 4 PM Thursday from New York.

Lots of love,

Tuesday afternoon   *Affectionately, Harold*

———

Editor's note: The letters in the next series cover a trip west in 1909 after a month and a half at home in Washington.

CONGRESS HOTEL, CHICAGO

July 4, 1909

My dearest Gertrude: I had a dusty trip today. It was a corker. It gave me a dust cold. Otherwise I am alright. I am in luck too. At the last minute some one gave up lower 13 to Seattle and I got it. I suppose they were afraid of the number. I am mighty glad as I hate an upper. I leave tonight at 10.15.

Pratt[61] met me at the station. He looks like McKay and seems like a fine fellow. I just got him off on the Santa Fe Limited. We had dinner

112

here. The big dining room was full of high rollers, sports of every description. I told him all about travel. He has never been in a sleeper.

I didn't like to leave Friday. I am going to get back as soon as I can. It will be some time in August. I will probably stop in Kansas on the way back and see several chicken packing houses with Miss Pennington. She will be making the shipments then. I want to know how the poultry is killed, and dressed and packed and handled. If she and her men are at work somewhere on the Santa Fe or near it, I will take the time to see it. It will help the work in the Department as I will know it then first hand and can help develop and protect it.

I hope you will get a good rest while the boys are away. It will be lonesome but it ought to be restful. Don't get too fat. I thought maybe the boys would be a little homesick when I took them off at Newark, but they didn't show any signs of it.

I have to write Josh and Taylor and I will drop the boys a note. Kiss the baby and tell him I held a little boy in my lap on the train today and told him about the Zoo. Good night, my dear. With much love

Affectionately, Harold

I took out an extra 5 day accident policy and enclose it.

───────

[Postcard postmarked St. Paul, July 5]

Have been walking around the town for 20 minutes. We have a half hour here and a few minutes across the river in Minneapolis. The best part is too far away from the station to see. There is a motley gang on the train. All sorts. Last winter in going to California I met Mr and Mrs Laird from Winona, Wis. He is a millionaire lumberman.[62] He came to see me at the Glenwood. They got on at Winona this morning and are going to Seattle on the same train. Love to you and Lawrence.

Harold

We are in Montana. It is like the high plains in Wyoming on the U.P. — a big unsettled grazing country. It is a cool trip. It wasn't dark last night till after nine. The sun was shining at 8.15 at Great Forks, N.Dak. Its a motley bunch on board. I am watching them and getting a good rest. Will be at Wenatchee at 12.20 tomorrow. Love to you and Lawrence.

Harold

━━━━━

[postcard postmarked Spokane, July 7]

Wednesday morning 7 oclock

We have just crossed the Montana line into Washington[63] and should be in Spokane now. There is a freight train off the track ahead of us so we cant tell how long the hold up will last. It is raining hard. I hope it dont rain in Wenatchee. Stuby will be there at 4.30 Last night we entered the Rockies at 7 'clock, reached the divide 5200 feet at 8.30. The ride down on this side was fine. It followed the Flathead River. It is not nearly as picturesque as the high Sierras on the Southern Pacific. The Cascades between Spokane and the coast are said to be fine. I wish you were here. It has been a delightfully cool trip. Love to you and Lawrence.

Harold

━━━━━

OLYMPIA HOTEL, WENATCHEE, WASH.

July 8, 1909 6,15 AM

My dearest Gertrude: We reached here 3 hours late yesterday afternoon and Stuby came later in the afternoon. It rained the night before coming through the mountains and was raining yesterday morning at Spokane. This is as dry as the desert here. There was a light rain night before last, the first in 9 months.

Wenatchee is on the Columbia River at the entrance to the Cascades. Between here and Spokane and the Rockies is a big plain called the Inland Empire. It is semi-arid and used for wheat. The apples here are in the Wenatchee valley which is above here and along the foothills west. Today we are going to drive out and see some of the growers and shippers and tomorrow we go 10 miles west to Cashmere or Calico, or some drygoods place, to see orchards there. Saturday morning we go to Seattle — 8 hours ride, and spend Sunday there, and Monday to Puyallup. From there about Friday we go back to Seattle for a couple of days and from the 19 to 21 at North Yakima, Wash. From the 21st to 24th probably at Hood River, Oregon. I cant tell beyond that. If you send letters to those places they will be forwarded if they do not reach me.

This is an interesting country. It is brown from the dry weather, rocky, black burned volcanic rocks. The Columbia is a winding river, running through almost rocky banks in many places. The people here are much like the New Castle type, pretty crude.[64] I do not think there are any problems here for us as the principal fruit is the winter apple.

Representative Cushman who was interested in having us come to Washington died of pneumonia day before yesterday. He was the humorist of the House and an able fellow. Paulhamus,[65] the chap who got us out here, wants to succeed him. He is a State Senator. Stuby is coming now to breakfast and I must stop. How are you getting along? I hope you are getting rested. It must be deadly monotonous though. How are the lilies? Tell me about the new ones when they come out. With much love to you and Lawrence. I have sent several postals to the boys.

Affectionately, Harold

———

Wenatchee, July 9, 1909

Dearest Gertrude: I was right glad to have your first letter last night and to hear that everything is going well. I hope you will have money enough to last. If you dont you will have to draw on the future by keeping back a little more of Taylor's loan. I am going to run short before I get through but will not draw on you. I will get some of Hosford or White or Shamel. I paid $8.00 for a double livery yesterday. Robbery!

115

Poor little Lawrence, he must be lonesome. I would like to have him in my arms now. I miss him very much as well as the rest of you.

Yesterday we drove around the valley and met a lot of growers. This morning we drive with two Chicago Commission men to Cashmere where there are a lot of fine orchards. We return this afternoon and leave at 5 tomorrow morning for Seattle. I wish you were here to take the Cascade trip with us. Stuby says the timber is magnificent. We were in an orchard of Winesaps yesterday that has net $2000 an acre for 3 yrs. The fruit growers here are the most ordinary looking men. They dont look as they could get the most out of money.

This is before breakfast at 6.15. We leave at 7 so I must go. Kiss and hug Lawrence for me and I send a lot of each to you.

Affectionately, Harold

———

HOTEL WASHINGTON ANNEX, SEATTLE

[postmarked July 11]

My dearest Gertrude: "Welcome to our city," "welcome friends," "welcome visitors," and "welcome, regular price $20. July price 11.67 1/2." The welcome sign is worked to the limit out here. They appear on everything and greet you everywhere. At Wenatchee there is a big semicircle over the street at the station in lights saying "Welcome to Wenatchee." The people look like it. They havent the finish of the Southern Californians.

We left at 5 o'clock this morning. The ride through the Cascades was a beautiful trip. The mountains are very heavily wooded with spruce, pine and firs — the heaviest and thickest timber I have seen on any of the mountains. The road follows a fierce foaming river a good deal of the way and there are some beautiful ribbon-like cascades in various canyons in which the white water can be seen from the top to the bottom of the mountain. It was foggy a good deal of the way so we didn't see the mts well.

It is raining here now. I have neither umbrella or coat. I suppose I will get a dollar umbrella and chuck it when I am through. Stuby and his brother and I are going to the exposition[66] this afternoon. We will stay here until Monday morning and then go to Puyallup, an hours

116

ride. I thought sure there would be some mail here today. I ordered it sent up from Puyallup. None has arrived yet. I am anxious to have my coat. I ought to have brought the raincoat too. It does not usually rain here in the summer, but they say it has rained a great deal this summer.

Sunday morning: Stuby's brother came in yesterday so I had to stop. We bought umbrellas and went to the Exposition. I worked most of the afternoon on our exhibit. The labels needed changing, and the boxes of models had to be rearranged. It is the government building. The general appearance of the exposition is fine. There are thousands and thousands of brilliant geraniums along each walk and the walks are usually below the geranium terraces on each side. I did not have time to go in any of the buildings except govt and agriculture. We are going again today and this afternoon go to Stubys brothers for dinner. His mother is there too. We went out last night.

There is no mail here yet. Seattle is hillier than San Francisco. It was too rainy yesterday to get much idea of the place. It is clear today. I wish you and the boys were here. I will go now. Stuby is waiting. With much love to you and a big hug for Lawrence.

Affectionately, Harold

═══════════

The Tacoma

Tacoma, Wash. July 12

Dearest Gertrude: I found your second letter at Puyallup this afternoon. I was glad to hear from you and to know that everything is alright. I hope Alice is getting the floors done without too much hard work. You could have the boy who helps Mrs Ashley if it is too hard. There must be at least a dozen coats of finish piled one on the other.

We saw lots of native spirea today like the one in the left hand border with the pink plumes. S. Belardie. It is a larger shrub and there are quantities of them. There are also beds of foxglove wild. They are 5 to 6 feet tall and dark colored. They are used in profusion in the decoration at the Fair and are very effective.

We were at the exposition yesterday and again this morning. It is a gem in artistic design and finish. It is far ahead of the others. The buildings are buff colored, but the greatest thing is the floral decorations. There are acres of pansies, or of pinks or of whatever flower is used.

I got in yesterday on my nerve and beauty. The ground opens at one o'clock. We didn't know it and were there at 9.30. I went to the outside administrative hall, presented my card, told them I wanted to work in the govt building, and was passed. Then I had to work in the govt building which is not open on Sunday. I rearranged a good deal of our exhibit and wrote a lot labels that are to be printed. Prof. Scribner who is in charge of all the exhibits in the Agr Dept took us over the grounds and explained the plan. I went in a number of buildings in the afternoon and several more this morning. I met Garstin and Leffers of Redlands and the Secy of the Chamber of Commerce in Riverside. I will go back and look over the labels to see if they are placed in the right places before I go.

Yesterday towards night Stub's brother took us across the Sound to a shack they have built on the beach. We had dinner there and came back by trolley. They are on the water and have a beautiful view. The shack has 5 rooms and probably didnt cost over $150 as lumber is cheap. It is very rough lumber. He built it himself. They have a baby 6 months old. Seattle is a beautifully located city on a range of rolling hills. It is situated somewhat like San Francisco but is more beautiful as the Sound and the three lakes in the city are wooded to the edge.

It is a great boost town. Everybody boosts. "welcome" appears everywhere—as long as you bring your pocket book. We will be at Puyallup till Friday and then go to Seattle for a couple of days. At North Yakima the 17–19 and Hood River, Oregon about the 21st to 23d. I will write other addresses later. You can send letters to Medford, Oregon about the 25th. I want to reach Sacramento by the 1st and leave California by the 8th. I think I will reach home between the 15th and 20th. We stop here and go to Puyallup every day by trolley. This is a fine hotel.

I must close now and write Taylor. Kiss Lawrence for me. With much love to you.

Affectionately, Harold

118

July 15

My Dearest Gertrude: We are on the move again. We came to Seattle last night by boat — two days ahead of schedule. Paulhamus who got us to come out came into line beautifully. He wanted work done and didnt know how to go about it. He was greatly pleased with the visit, entirely satisfied, and he is going to write both the Secretary and Dr Galloway. He is a hustling, pushing westerner with lots of progressive ideas, and probably with not too much principle. Anything to win. He could probably be U.S. Senator or governor. He started an investigation of the present state offices. The attorney general resigned, the Treasurer is in jail, and the insurance commissioner is headed that way. He cant help bossing things. He goes up stairs three steps at a time and slides down the bannister or jumps over the railing. He has a beautiful farm and a crack dairy. Yesterday he brought a pint of thick cream and we had it with raspberries at lunch. I have eaten quarts of real raspberries. I have thought of you and wished you were here to enjoy them as well as the other things.

The trip last night was fine. We left at 7.30 and the gigantic mountain Rainer, or Tacoma as it is called locally, loomed up alone far into the sky and filled the eastern horizon at a distance from the end of the harbor. It was already warming up in color and as the sun went down it was all aglow with purples and pinks and grays and all sorts of colors. It is a grand mountain. It is the kind I pictured as a boy — a great enormous, solitary rugged peak, all covered with snow. It rises out of the Cascades and they seem pigmies in comparison. After three quarters of an hour when it was shut out of view, I turned my chair and watched a brilliant sunset. Across a large part of it the jagged edges of the Olympia range broke the skyline. They were indigo blue. The contrast between them and the golden sky was magnificent. It reminded me a little of the beautiful sunset I saw in going out of the Bay of Naples to Messina.

We will be at the Exposition today and go to North Yakima tomorrow. We need the extra days as there are several places we will have to see between there and Hood River. We will be at Portland, Portland Hotel, the 25th at Medford Oregon, the 28th and at 2747 Woolsey St Berkeley the 31st and 1st. I will probably go to Los

119

Angeles the night of the 1st. You can send mail after that to the Hayward until about the 4th and then to the Glenwood.

It must be a hard job to get the floors in shape. It will be still harder down stairs as there are more coats on. You ought to get the boy to help and not do it yourself when it comes to the filler. We will appreciate them when it is done. They will need scrubbing and sandpapering down stairs to get the wood smooth.

I think I will send this to Coochs Bridge as you will probably be there in two or three days. Give them all my love. I wish I could be there with you. We would have a good time. I would rather have you here. I am enjoying the trip very much. I am afraid I am no more of a fairy than when I started. I suspect I am less so. If fishes are fattening I'll be fit to kill soon. Stuby and I had a baked salmon trout night before last that was the most delicious fish I ever ate. It was 18 inches long, cooked to a turn, pink and juicy. I thought of you and wished for you. My love to you and the boys.

Affectionately, Harold

On the train to Yakima, July 16

Dearest Gertrude: We have crossed the Cascades and are inland in the arid country again. We will be in N. Yakima in half an hour. We will recross the Cascades on the way back to Portland. This will make 3 crossings. We are following the Yakima River now. It looks very different from the humid climate we left this morning. The trip through the mountains was fine but not as good as the Great Northern. This is the Northern Pacific. I think we will be at Portland by the 23d and at Medford Oregon by the 26th instead of the 28th. Stubys the 30 or 31st.

Taylor wires he has sent a lot of important letters to me at Seattle and that I will have to help Dennis with some Civil Service papers — a lot of money matters. He is sick and is on the coast. I hope it wont delay me.

I am sending an expense account to Taylor for about $90 and have asked him to get it to you as soon as possible. If you are at Coochs Bridge mail it to the bank. I will need to draw on it a little after the

1st. I have $100 left but it takes about $50 a week. Dont draw on this after it is deposited.

I want to mail this on the train so I will stop. I was at the Exposition yesterday. I stayed last night and heard Lamberti's band. I wished you were there. Seattle is allright. They are great boosters but they have a spirit that is building up a fine city. I went through most of the buildings yesterday. At one exhibit they gave us a whole box of big black cherries and told us to "go to it" and we did double quick.

Love to all the folks and the boys. I wish I were with you.

Affectionately, Harold

———

HOTEL VILLARD   PASCO   WASH

July 16

My Dearest Gertrude: We are ahead of our schedule. We will be in Hood River tomorrow and next day, 19th and 20th; Portland 21st; Salem, Oregon 22d, Berkeley 26 and 27. Los Angeles Probably 28 or 29th. So you had better start mail towards the Hayward. I got two letters at Yakima yesterday from Seattle. I dont see how the 30 overdraw happened. It must be in the tangle of last winter's accts. Mr Taylor will let you have the money. I am getting on well with personal expenses. I am about $6 or $8 out personally so far. I dont want the trip to run over $25.

This is a junction point. We got here at 2 AM and leave in a few minutes at 8 AM for Pendleton, Ore. Then at 12 noon we go to Umatilla and drive from there this afternoon to Hermiston to the Reclamation project; back to Umatilla and leave there at 3.30 AM for Hood River. This is strenuous. Yesterday we drove all morning and went 50 miles in an auto in the afternoon in clouds of dust and addressed the Commercial Club in the evening.

The Yakima Valley is an enormous county. There are 12000 acres of apples in bearing and 35000 planted and 500,000 acres under the irrigation projects. The valley is being settled by a class of people more like Southern California than any place I have seen. There are fine homes, high priced orchard $2000 to 2500 an acre and a booster spirit. The main valley is round and about ten miles in diameter.

There are several small valleys that radiate out from it. All of them are being planted to apples rapidly.

The growers and shippers are very anxious to have us extend our work there. There were a lot of them at the Commercial Club last night. They are going to take it up with the Secretary and with their Senator who lives at North Yakima. We can do them a lot of good. I cant write more now. Lots of love to the boys and you and to Lee and Marian and Margaret.

Affectionately, Harold

_____

Hermiston, Oregon
Monday July 19

My Dearest Gertrude: We are hung up here and lose the day. We got here from Umatilla yesterday afternoon and drove over the project. We thought of going at 12.45 AM but my head began to ache at night and I had a splitter for a few hours. I have never had but two or three such and they come when I am travelling hard, losing sleep and over-eating. I have to sit up as the top of my head nearly lifts off when I lie down. I had a much worse one in London last fall.[67] It has stopped now but I feel like going easy. We were to take a train from Hood River at 10 but it doesnt get here till 12.45 and may be still later. We will probably reach Hood River by 6 this afternoon. I am going a little slower from now on.

This is a God-forsaken country. It is all sand and sagebrush. There are 25000 acres in the project when the sagebrush is cleared your farm is likely to get busy and you find it the next day in some adjoining county or scattered over several of them. Potatoes blow out of the ground and beets may be left without any soil around them. This is where the soil is improperly handled. I cant see why the government should spend $60 an acre reclaiming such land when there are millions of acres of better soil for agricultural purposes. The reclamation work as a whole is one of the greatest public services ever undertaken, but every once in a while you find a project that is located because some nice engineering work can be done rather than for its agricultural value after it is finished. The price of land is ridiculously high. They ask $75 to $150 an acre for these sand heaps.

We had a long trip yesterday. Some of it through the hilly hard wheat country was very interesting. We expected to miss connections at Pendleton for Umatilla, but the train from the east was 15 minutes late so we just made it. Otherwise we would have been hung up there all day.

The weather has been delightfully cool all over the northwest. It is usually 100 or more here but I dont think it is over 90. We havent had any hot days.

I am at the Reclamation office. I have a lot of correspondence to attend to so here I send my love to all of you Cooches and boys and you.

Affectionately, Harold

―――――――――

[July 20?]

My Dearest Gertrude: Your good letter of the 13th came this morning and I was glad to hear from you. You are at Marian's now. Don't hurry home just to get the wax on. You ought to have at least 10 days there. I think Taylor will need all of his money when the 1st comes. His insurance is due next month and in a letter from him a day or two ago he said he had let you have the money and that he would not need it this month. Send to Father for it if you need it. I enjoyed the clipping from Jeffrey. It was very modestly put, Stuby says I deserve more but there are limits to the English language.

I am counting on the Ghent trip. We ought to have a fine time. We will stay two weeks and maybe three if they can take care of us. We will try to get in some good drives. I dont want to see an apple or talk trees, but I'll help Baby pick apples, drive with you, or do anything else.

White has turned turtle and wants to resign. He is a spoiled kid. I am going to accept it. He wants to pull out Sept 15 just at the beginning of the Watsonville work which was planned for him. He is sore because he didnt get a salary raise. I'll not baby him this time. We have twice before. I am sorry you will miss the lilies. I would like to see them.

We had a beautiful trip along the Columbia yesterday. This town is down by the river and the valley is up on the hill. It is the most famous apple valley in the country. We drove 30 miles in it today. Mt Hood is at one end, big and sharp and white and at the opposite side of the river far back is Mt Adams. Both are white the year around and both are magnificent mountains.

Tomorrow we cross the river to White Salmon, Wash. We come back in the afternoon and take a boat at 5 to Portland. The Columbia is the most picturesque river I ever saw. The banks are high and rocky, the current is rapid and often foamy. We will get in at 9. Thursday we are in some orchards near Portland. Friday at Salem and back to Portland at night, and Saturday to Medford, Sunday en route Monday at Lodi. Tuesday and Wednesday at Berkeley and Thursday at Los Angeles. Hayward Hotel. You can send all mail there.

I am tired tonight so I must close. I have lost 2 shirts, 6 collars, a pair of pajamas, handkerchiefs and a set of underwear. The laundry didnt come back in time to Tacoma. The package was to be sent but it hasnt been yet. I may get it. Lots of love to you and the boys and all.

Affectionately, Harold

———————

Mt Hood Hotel   Hood River Oregon

July 21

My Dearest Gertrude: We are just leaving for Portland on the boat. How I wish you were here to take the trip. The river is magnificently grand in scenery. This morning we crossed to White Salmon and climbed the hill 2000 feet to a big plateau. There are thousands of acres of apple orchards just planted in the cleared land. The country is heavily timbered with pine. It is more pioneer than anything we have been in. With 5000 to start with you can easily increase your investment to 20000 in 5 years in the increased value of improvements. The thing to do is to buy 20 acres or 40 at 125 an acre. It costs 150 an acre to clear and plant it. At 5 years it is easily worth 1000 an acre and ought to pay 20% on that valuation. We enjoyed the drive very much. We had to walk 2 miles back as the wagon broke. It was hot and dusty.

I must scoot. Love to you all.

Affectionately, Harold

Portland Oregon   July 22

My Dearest Gertrude: We had a beautiful trip on the Columbia last night. The ride for three hours through the Cascades was wild and mountainous as the most rugged part of the Hudson trip. We got in at 9.30. The hotels here are filled to overflowing. We wired a day ahead and slept on cots in a sample room. Tonight we will have a better room. I made all arrangements to be at Salem this morning and then left it to Stuby to look up trains and to make all arrangements here. He came to me and said it was time to go. I looked at my watch and found it was within 10 minutes of train time and the station a mile and a half away. Of course we couldn't make it. I had to get busy on the phone and change all the plans. We stay here today and go to Salem tomorrow. I have a lot of letters to dictate and a big orchard to visit near here this afternoon, so it doesnt make much difference. We take the train tomorrow night from Salem to Medford and reach there Saturday at 10.41 AM. Leave Sunday morning at 10.45 on the same train for Sacramento. Then to Lodi and to Berkeley Wednesday and Los Angeles Thursday. Lots of love to you all.

Affectionately, Harold

HOTEL NASH   MEDFORD OREGON

July 25 1909

My Dearest Gertrude: We reached here yesterday noon and were met by a delegation of fruit men. In the afternoon they took us all over the Rogue River Valley. It is a big section and the Bartlett pear and winter apple are the two leading fruits. They grow the finest pears in the country here. Last night I spoke nearly 2 hours at the Commercial Club. The day before the Board of Trade at Salem met us and the Mayor and four automobiles took us over the Salem district. We are having a great trip, mighty interesting and strenuous. We leave this morning for Sacramento. I think Stuby has arranged for some blow out at Lodi tomorrow. He hasn't said much about it but I am looking for an auto delegation.

I found three letters here from you and was mighty glad to hear from you. I haven't time now to make any comments as a Mr Whisler is coming in a few minutes with a machine to take us to a big orchard before train. I had about a dozen letters from Taylor. Please mail a couple of blank checks at once. As soon as the expense account is deposited I want to draw on it and have no checks. Send to Los Angeles Hayward Hotel and send all other mail there.

I must close now. Give much love and kisses to the boys and have them give you some for me.

Affectionately, Harold

Berkeley   July 27
[postmarked San Jose, July 29]

My Dearest Gertrude: We got here this morning and I am going to stay till tomorrow noon. Then I go to San Jose to see about a cooperative movement among the prune people and to Los Angeles at night. I will be there Thursday morning. I have a lot of work to do there. Dennis has a whole lot of mixed accounts that have to be straightened out and 90 papers to look over for the Civil Service. He is careless about finances. There is one bill of over 1000 and another of 400 that were rendered last November for work on the one car.[68] He has let them go and the firms have taken it up directly with the Secretary. I am going over all of the vouchers and bring things up to date. I realize now that Dennis has been overworked and that he lacks executive ability. He needs a manager.

I had a letter from Taylor saying that Galloway and Wiley were both much in favor of bringing all of the storage and transportation work closer together. Miss Pennington will be in the middle west when I return with several assistants and she will plan out a trip so that three or four of us can take in a number of the big packing establishments. I imagine it will take a week and I want to reach there before the 10th, so I ought to get home between the 18th and the 20th. We will leave as soon as I can for Ghent. It will take a few days to straighten things out in Washington. Maybe we can stay away three weeks.

The War Dept wants the Agr. Dept to send some one to the Canal

Zone in Panama to see what fruits are adapted there. Galloway wants either (Mrs Stuby says tell Mrs Powell I am just as giddy as I ever was and haven't improved a bit. She says I am very lovely and am getting prettier every day) Taylor or me to go. I am going to pass it. It will do Taylor good to make the trip. If we had some way of leaving the children and could go together it would be different. We could have a fine trip.

Stuby changes completely as soon as he gets home. He gets quiet and irritable, tells the children not to do this or that to which they pay no attention. Arnold is a big silly kid. He is a fine boy but has reached the silly boy stage. Mrs Stuby and Bailey are well.

I am going over to the university this afternoon. Stuby is developing some films we took on the trip. We have made about 120 exposures. I have some good ones of the exposition.

I must close now and write Taylor. Lots of love to you and the boys.

Affectionately, Harold

HOTEL ST JAMES, SAN JOSE

July 29, 1909

My Dearest Gertrude: I have just a minute before going to the train for Los Angeles. I came here this noon to look into a prune association. I will be in Los Angeles in the morning.

I imagine you did not send a letter to Stuby's and that I will find one at the Hayward tomorrow. Don't use Hayward or Glenwood paper in writing to those places.

You ought to see Stuby's and Mrs Stuby's discipline. One tells the kid one thing and the other another. They discuss all his good and bad traits before him and try to make him mind by scaring him. This morning they opened a cupboard door so "Mr Brown" would come and get him. He didn't mind Mr Brown any but the way he yelled at his mother to shut that door was a caution. His father told him he couldn't have an apple under any circumstances. Arny asked his mother if he could have one, so he got it. Our discipline or rather yours is perfect in comparison.

Time to go so here's love to you and the boys.

Affectionately, Harold

My Dearest Gertrude: I got in this morning a couple of hours late. All of the boys, Shamel, Hosford, Pratt, and McKay were here. White was somewhere else. I will see him tomorrow. I have had a talk with Dennis and he will come to Riverside Monday night. He says he is much better.

I came down on the train with Mr Sechrist, the Gen'l Mgr. of the Pacific Fruit Express. He is a great supporter of our work. He has the car lines on all the Harriman systems.

I found your letter written Friday. I hope Clark has got rested and that you are all well. You must have had a fine trip. Did you get any rest? Give my love and a kiss to Frances. I would like to see her. I am going to see Mr James, the Exchange attorney, this afternoon about the legal sides of cooperatives.

Shamel is waiting so I will run. I try to get a note off every day. Give lots of love to the boys and a big hug all around.

Affectionately, Harold

My Dearest Gertrude: I was at San Dimas, Claremont and Pomona yesterday. Woodford is not very well. — liver balky — and is home for a few days. I took lunch with him. I drove to Claremont-Pomona and saw Mr Dreher[69] and came back here at night. All the boys were here, Rolfs, the Director of the Florida station will be here today to look into the withertip fungus, a bad trouble in the lemon. Walraff is at the Glenwood. Lyman will be here today on their way to Oregon where they camp. I will take lunch with them. There is a meeting of the Lemon Mens Club at the Chamber of Commerce today at which Hosford gives a summary of the lemon work. It will be a good sized meeting and Rolfs and I will also hold forth.

I go to Riverside this afternoon and will be there till Wednesday. Mr Chase called up last night and wants me to stay at their house. He says the house and automobile are at my disposal. I will probably stay there till Monday. Dennis comes up Monday night from Laguna and I will be tied up with him Tuesday. The Exchange matter is all off so far as I am concerned. There is considerable opposition to the plan on the part of some of the Association managers who are afraid they will lose their jobs. Under these circumstances I wouldn't undertake it. It would be too risky. Woodford was all stirred up and is yet, and came near resigning.

Love to all of you. Send the next letter to Springfield, Mo. I will be there some time early next week.

Affectionately, Harold

Riverside, Aug. 1, 1909
[written at the home of Ethan
Allen Chase and postmarked Aug. 2]

My Dearest Gertrude: I slept on the porch last night. I have a big bed in the room and another outside. It is fine to be able to sleep out. I don't blame you for wanting to do it. They have a canvas about 3 feet high all around on the porch railing. I will go to the Glenwood tomorrow as it is more convenient to meet the boys there. It is a fine let up here. I have a summer cold and am all stopped up in my head. I don't know where I got it. We are going to Redlands, Oak Glen and Beaumont this morning. Walraff is going too. Lots of love to you from the Chases and me and to the boys.

Affectionately, Harold

GLENWOOD MISSION INN
[Postmarked Riverside Aug 2]

My Dearest Gertrude: Here I am again and the dinners and banquets have already begun. I thought my dinner coat was a heavy weight all the way around but tomorrow it gets polished and put on. Mr Reed has just been in and he wants to invite about a dozen men in to meet me at dinner tomorrow. Stuby and Shamel and Rolfs will be called in as properly distributed satellites. The Glenwood will bring out its oldest wine. I am turning down dinners every few minutes. Can't take time from my official duties. Too busy.

I went into the telegraph office to send a message this morning and was greeted by Miss Garlick of Newark. She is playing the keyboard here. It took courage but I fell on her neck and got an onion kiss.

Yesterday Mr Chase, Frank, Walraff and I went to Redlands, Eucaipa,[70] Oak Glen, way over to San Jacinto mountain and back home — 80 miles.

I won't send for my laundry. It is is at North Yakima with an express bill to pay. It would cost $1.50 to get it here. As the shirts are old they can keep them. I bought three new ones instead. I forgot to bring a white shirt so I will have to buy one.

I am glad Frances is with you. I like to give her one with only onions in it. Give her my love and lots to you and the boys. I am working with Dennis today.

Affectionately, Harold

GLENWOOD

[postmarked Aug 4]

My Dearest Gertrude: The banquet was a success. There were about twenty — J. H. Reed, Harry and Frank and Mr Chase, Rumsey, Moulton, H. O. Reed, Prof Norton,[71] Zumbro,[72] Stuby, Shamel, Fred Reed, Rolfs, Frank Miller, Dennis, Mr Waite, Charters, Call. We began at seven and sat at the table till eleven. There were eloquent speeches by myself, Shamel, Rolfs and Mr Chase. Mr Reed of course was toast master and was in a happy frame of mind. The dinner was given for Shamel and your lovely husband.

I am working hard with Dennis and have all of the accounts straightened out except one big one which we will finish this morning. Then we tackle 90 Civil Service papers. I will leave here at noon tomorrow for Los Angeles and will spend the night with Shamel at Pasadena. I took dinner yesterday at the Handy's. Dennis called her "the little girl" and I almost slid in like a drinking cup. That's scandalous language from Dennis.

Tell George I was glad to have his letter. I will pull his teeth out when I get home. I am glad the boys have a tent. I am drawing a check for $85 this morning — my last account. I sent in an account of 105 yesterday. Don't touch it. Its poison and belongs to Eustace.

I leave on the Limited Friday for Wichita Kan and will be there Monday. I don't know the schedule after that. Send me a letter there. Give lots of love to the boys and to Frances and you.

Wednesday 7 A.M.   *Affectionately, Harold*

August 5

My Dearest Gertrude: I have your letter and the blank checks. I had a blank check from Hosford on the same bank, so I had drawn 85 before they came. There must have been a few cents disallowed as the account was 85.02. The trip has not been very expensive for me. Up to date am out only $5.00 If I can get through with $10 on personal expense I will do well. I bought three shirts and some stockings.

I go to Los Angeles this morning at 11.25 and spend the night with Shamel at Pasadena and leave in the morning at 10 on the Limited, spend Sunday night at Newton, Kansas, reach Wichita Kan Monday morning at 7.45 There about 3 days. Then to Springfield Mo. Thursday and Friday, leave there Saturday for Chicago and spend Monday with a carload of precooled poultry sent from Springfield.

Miss Pennington has a trip to Keokuk Iowa planned for Tuesday but I think I will cut that out unless there is some new method of handling there. I want to become thoroughly familar with all of the details of handling on this trip. This ought to bring me home by the 20th or a day or two before. I have written Taylor that we want to leave as soon as I get the trip straightened out for Ghent. I am going to try for a three weeks leave.

You will find an account of the dinner in the Press. It states it was given for Shamel and Rolfs. I passed it up to them as the Press man came to see me about it and so I gave him the account he published. It was a nice affair.

Yesterday Dr and Mrs Davenport and their little girl were here. He is a [?] and director in Illinois. Stuby was to be there and Shamel is a graduate I had Mr Chase take them out in the morning and Mr Rumsey in the afternoon. I have had a very busy time here straightening out Dennis's accounts. I landed Rumsey of Whittier for our work yesterday. He is a fine fellow. It will make the Berkeley people roar. He comes in Oct 15. Dennis has just come in to finish the acct. I have all of your letters and am afraid I will miss a number from now on. I am anxious to get home and wish the Kansas and Missouri trips would be put off. It seems to be the time to do it. With a great deal of love to you and the boys and Frances.

Affectionately, Harold

Friday morning
68 N. Los Robles St
Pasadena
[postmarked Aug 7]

My Dearest Gertrude: I am at Shamels. They have a cottage apartment, 2 floors belonging to some artist, opposite the Maryland. The Hosfords were here to dinner last night and White and Pratt came in for the evening. They have a little girl — a dear little thing a year old. Mrs Shamel is a pleasant girl, large and fine looking. She is as tall as Shamel and some day will be like Mother.

I leave at 10 this morning. It is going to be a hot ride today. It was about a hundred yesterday and was growing warmer. The ride from Riverside was like a furnace, but when we reached Los Angeles it was delightful, with a cool breeze. Los Angeles is a good deal cooler than the interior. I imagine it will be way over a hundred at the Needles. I have a lower and wont mind it. I hope there will be no nice looking girl in the upper to whom I will have to give my lower. Did I write you how I got one on Stuby?

Coming down from Oregon I had lower 2 and he lower 1. There was a man in my upper and a very attractive blond had Stuby's upper. Stuby looked her over and decided she was about 18 and then he began to growl. "She's younger than I am and she's got to climb up." He growled all day. Finally we got in conversation. She was a charming schoolteacher and older than her pink complexion showed. After a while I got an opening and I said, "I am very sorry you haven't my upper so *I* could have the pleasure of giving you *my* lower." Poor old Stuby, he had to come through and give it up. Then I told her I had been urging him all day to give her the lower, that he was a woman hater, and that he had to be forced to show them any attention. Did I write about the lady whose chair tipped over on the boat coming down the Columbia? She fell on my shoulder and it was so funny I never touched her. She was flustered and asked rather sharply why I didn't help her up to which I responded, "Why should I?" That set Stuby and the party with her in a gale and we exchanged gibes all the way to Portland. It is breakfast time. I hope some blondes chair will tip over on the Limited. Love . . . The Shamels, Hosfords, Chases, Frank Miller, Reed, Woodford sent regards

Affectionately, Harold

THE HAMILTON, WICHITA, KANSAS

Aug 9, 1909

My Dearest Gertrude: I have been initiated into the chicken business today. We spent all day at a packing house watching them kill and dress hundreds of chickens. The difficulties are not unlike the fruit troubles of broken skin, bruises from rough handling, water cooling which is like the washing of oranges, slow cooling, dirt, etc.

Of course I must have an automobile ride so tomorrow morning a Mr Woods takes me out 10 miles to see a big apple orchard. The rest of the day will be spent in watching chickens packed that were killed today. They are cooling tonight. We go on a sleeper to Topeka tomorrow night and go Thursday night on one to Springfield and to Chicago Saturday night by sleeper. Monday and Tuesday will be spent with the shipments put up here and at Topeka and Wednesday at Carrolton, Mo. I will be home by Saturday at the latest. I got your Aug. 1 letter from Riverside here today. The trip to Ghent ought to brace Clark up and it may be cooler by that time.

I am tired tonight. My room last night was in the Harvey Hotel at Newton right on the track. The cars were going by every few minutes and it seemed as though I didn't sleep an hour. Mr Safford, Miss Pennington's young chemist, is a nice fellow.

I am going to bed. I have a million chicken crawlers on me and I have got to drown them. With lots of love to all of you.

Affectionately, Harold

The National Hotel, Topeka, Kansas

Aug 11 1909

My Dearest Gertrude: Hot as Hades and no let up in sight. It was 95 yesterday and last night was a hot one. We leave this afternoon at 2.15 and leave Kansas City at 6.15 reaching Springfield at 12 tonight. We thought that was better than a sleeper.

Last night we had a dinner at the Elks Club by Mr Bowman, The Pres. of the Seymour Packing Co. The special feature was a delicious broiler for each.

The plant here is a good one, more in the Chase class. The one at Wichita was pretty bad. This poultry problem is one of the prettiest I ever saw.

I started to write a note last night but the perspiration was in streams and I chucked the job. This is before breakfast. I hope it is not any hotter with you. Give much love to the boys and Frances if she is still there. With much love to you.

Affectionately, Harold

United States Packing Co.
Butter, eggs, and poultry, Chicago
Springfield, Mo, branch.

Aug 14

My Dearest Gertrude: There is one satisfaction in working in this chicken business in hot weather, nearly all of the places have cooling rooms in which you can go when the heat raises the lid. It is very hot. I have slept without a sheet, nightie or anything else several nights. It is rather trying on the eyes of the chamber maids when they come in before you are awake as one did yesterday, but still art is always good to look at.

Miss Pennington and Stafford are getting a shipment ready this morning to go this afternoon. I never saw her equal as an indefatigable worker. She goes like a house afire all day and gets what she is after. I am getting a good deal out of the trip along the precooling lines. We leave for Chicago tonight and reach there tomorrow night via Kansas City. Monday and Tuesday we are on the receiving work and the laboratory and my railroad men. Tuesday night to Carrollton Mo. and I leave there so as to be home Friday. I don't know what time as I cant tell till after we get there.

This poultry deal is a hard nut to crack. Most of them are way below the worst of the orange packers. They are not organized and they are hard to reach.

Yesterday I was rather out of commission with a bloodshot eye. I caught cold on the train Thursday night. I have put boric acid in it every half hour or so and it is better today.

I am out of money. I will wire Taylor Monday to see if the last expense account is in. If it isn't I will have to draw $25 on the salary. So please hold that back if the account isnt it. I must close now. I will be glad to be home again. With much love to all.

Affectionately, Harold

ELMS HOTEL, CHICAGO

Aug 15

My Dearest Gertrude: We got here this noon after a scorching trip. We left Springfield yesterday afternoon and just made the Santa Fe Limited last night at Kansas City. We had 20 minutes for the change and were 20 minutes late. We ran around trains, knocked over passengers and just made it. The ride from Springfield was very dirty.

Drs St. John and Witmer, two of Miss Pennington's woman assistants, are here, also Stafford and Dr Somebody else. Tomorrow I will be in the R.R. yards and laboratory, Tuesday in the laboratory and Wednesday in the chicken houses here. I will leave Wednesday afternoon sometime and will be home Thursday unless something occurs here. Miss Pennington has already hit a big lead. She has been getting the percentage of chickens in which the blood showed in the neck and wing arteries. In the best house in the West — Topeka she found 48%. These chickens go to pieces in a hurry so she sent a lot here and yesterday the girls found the trouble after dissecting all of them. It is God [?] — all the arteries were not cut in killing. This is due to piece killing and hurry work.

Tomorrow I will help lay out a series of experiments on properly and improperly killed birds. This is as important as our clipper cutting. She is naturally greatly elated over it as the results of the experiments will be clear cut, and the trouble can be corrected.

I got a letter here written Aug 3 and one Aug 9 and was glad to have them. I am curious about that mysterious present on the mantle. I hope there wont be a hitch in the vacation plans. I suspect Taylor wants to go to Michigan as soon as he can. We will have to divide the time as he will have to go before school closes. The trouble is there is no one to leave in charge when we are away. I slept till 8.30 this morning. I sleep better on a car than any where else. The motion of the car keeps me asleep.

This is a splendid family hotel on the lake in Hyde Park and 53d st. I am sorry Harold and Emma are not here. I will call up the Gardiners later and will go over this evening if they are home. It must be hot in Washington. I will let you know by wire when I arrive and if it is not too late you can come down.

I have a really pathetic letter from Woodford. He is greatly disappointed that I am not there. I told him he couldn't bring it up again as there are some who do not want it.

Lovingly, Harold

Editor's note: Woodford did bring it up again, and late in the following year he prevailed. Powell left government service to work for the growers, first as secretary and general manager of the Citrus Protective League, a subsidiary of the California Fruit Growers Exchange and then in 1912 to be general manager of the Exchange itself.

As his letters make clear, Powell needed a larger income, which government tradition and policy denied him. His move from government at $3000 to the Exchange at $10,000 illustrates a problem serious in 1910 as in 1990, the loss of skilled government personnel to the private sector of the economy. The New York Tribune on April 9, 1911, carried a long piece, "Uncle Sam to Yield His Scientists in Aid of Business," on Federal men in wheat rust, sugar, drainage, artesian wells, crop growing, and pomology lost to better-paying private employers.

After a decade and a half of scientific service to the public, Powell had left Uncle Sam for Sunkist. The Eastern deciduous fruit expert, a star in the Bureau of Plant Industry, became a citrus expert in the evergreen groves of the Golden West. And now he became an economic and political executive prominent in commercial enterprise on the national scene.

NOTES FOR THE LETTERS OF 1909

1. B. A. Woodford, General Manager of the California Fruit Growers Exchange, July, 1904, to September 1912, when Powell succeeded him. He was a business man, a banker, and a lemon grower in Ontario and Cucamonga—one of five who organized the Lemon Growers Exchange of Ontario.

2. Harry B. Chase, one of Ethan Allen's sons, President of the Chase Rose Co. In 1906 he became the first vice-president of the Citrus Protective League.

3. Lyman V. W. Brown, son of Judge E. G. Brown, orange grower and owner of a famous estate called Anchorage, was President of the Rivino Water Co., Vice-president of La Sierra Water Co., and very active in local affairs such as the big agricultural convention of March, 1909.

4. Frank Chase, active in the management of the Chase orchards.

5. During the winters of 1905, 1906, and 1907, the Powell family rented part of the home of Miss Handy and her brother Ben. The Handys had moved west from Marion, Massachusetts.

6. Lawrence Chase Powell, later Lawrence Clark Powell.

7. Stubenrauch, now a close family friend. According to Gertrude he played a good piano—Chopin and Strauss waltzes.

8. Dr. and Mrs. Wilson and their daughter Anne, 22 years old, lived in Pasadena.

9. Eureka, an orchard district. Eurekas, lemons.

10. Among others, "the boys" included G. W. "Mac" McKay and C. M. Pomeroy, each an Assistant in Lemon Studies. Josh, whom the Powells were sending money to, remained unidentifiable in 1989 by either Lawrence Clark Powell or retired scientists in the U.S.D.A.'s Agricultural Research Service.

11. Cornelius Earle Rumsey (?).

12. Beverly T. Galloway, pathologist and physiologist, Chief of the Bureau of Plant Industry.

13. H. M. White, Scientific Assistant in Fruit Marketing, Transportation, and Storage Investigations.

14. Charles Morgridge Loring, born in Maine, went westward for health to Minneapolis, where he became a success as a merchant, miller, and dealer in real estate. He became a national figure in civic betterment. From the 1880s on he spent winters in Riverside, where he built the Opera House and helped make Mt. Rubidoux into a city park.

15. "When Sec. Wilson first took office, the department of agriculture was still something of a joke; today it is one of the greatest and most useful departments of the government. Mr. Wilson has organized its work on scientific and businesslike lines and he has called about him a body of capable men whose scientific researches and practical work in behalf of the agricultural interests of the country have compelled the admiration of the world." *The Riverside Press,* March 7, 1909.

16. John F. Boal, Manager of the San Diego Land & Town Co.

17. R. C. Allen, a fruit grower and packer.

18. Bartlett Richards, "a wealthy cattle man and banker of Nebraska," spent winters at his home in Coronado. *San Diego Union,* March 8, 1901. He was president and treasurer of the California Lemon Co. in National City.

19. Answer: a ring lovers wear to signify remembrance. By March 23 Powell had answered his own question.

20. In 1909 there were seventeen district exchanges, each of which included numerous local associations, companies, and exchanges. Rahno Mabel MacCurdy: *The History of the California Fruit Growers Exchange* (Los Angeles, 1925), pp. 67–68.

21. Archibald Dixon Shamel (1878–1956), Investigator in Plant Breeding. He had shown that by bud selection people could produce pedigreed fruit trees analogous to pedigreed livestock. The Bureau sent Shamel west largely through Powell's influence, to work on lemons. J. H. Reed saw pedigreed trees as adding to the value of orchards by at least twenty-five percent.

22. The University of California, the State Horticultural Commission, and the Southern Pacific Railroad Co. sponsored the Agricultural and Horticultural Train, which stopped in farming centers to show instructive exhibits and to provide talks by professors on topics such as citrus culture, citrus pests, care and culture of various soils, handling of cover crops, tree and plant diseases, and tuberculosis in cows. *Los Angeles Times,* March 13, 1909.

23. Dr. C. Van Zwalenburg, a director on both Riverside banks.

24. Charles H. Low, Vice-president of the Security Savings Bank, Riverside, and a director of the Citizens National Bank.

25. G. N. Reynolds, formerly with the National Biscuit Co., now a prominent grower.

26. J. W. Jeffrey, State Horticultural Commissioner.

27. Edward J. Wickson, Dean of the College of Agriculture at the University of California in Berkeley, 1907–1912.

28. Harry J. Eustace, Expert in Fruit Storage, among the five men who assisted Powell in preparing Bulletin 123.

29. Harold Haines Clark, Gertrude's brother, working in Chicago for the Link-Belt Company.

30. The Loring dinner in the Mission Inn was laid for eighteen, the decorations in flags and oranges. *The Riverside Press,* March 17, 1909.

31. Eustace gave the nickname Tommy to Lawrence.

32. James Dennis, Expert in Refrigeration. He devised the portable refrigeration plant for freight cars, "which contributed very largely to the cold storage and pre-cooling work in the early days of research in this field. . . ." H. P. Gould, Bureau of Fruit and Vegetable Crop Diseases, Beltsville, Maryland, February 26, 1942. Powell Papers, Box 9, Folder 6. Dennis designed the first U.S.D.A. experimental refrigerated car, exhibited in Riverside on April 13, 1909.

33. J. F. Fernald, an assistant in the lemon work.

34. Mt. Rubidoux, a rocky hill to the west of Riverside, rising 500 feet above the Santa Ana River.

35. Dr. Herbert John Webber (1865–1946), a pathologist at the U.S.D.A. Experiment Station in Eustis, Florida, and later Professor of Subtropical Agriculture at, and Director of, the Citrus Experiment Station in Riverside.

36. L. S. Tenny, Pomologist in Fruit Marketing, Transportation, and Storage Investigations.

37. Albert F. Woods, Pathologist and Physiologist and Assistant Chief of the Bureau of Plant Industry.

38. E. M. Chace, Assistant Chief of the Division of Foods, Bureau of Chemistry, U.S.D.A., author of "The By-Products of the Lemon in Italy," Bulletin 160 (1909). For several months Powell consistently misspelled his name.

39. Dr. Mary Engle Pennington, Chief of the Food Research Laboratory, Bureau of Chemistry, U.S.D.A.

40. Dr. Harvey W. Wiley, Chief Chemist, U.S.D.A.

41. Packing houses stood at Prenda, the terminus of a spur of the Santa Fe tracks.

42. George Thompson, retired editor of the *St. Paul Dispatch.*

43. Walter Tennyson Swingle, E. Sc., Pathologist in Charge of Plant Life-history Investigations.

44. G. W. Hosford, Assistant Pomologist in Fruit Marketing, Transportation, and Storage Investigations, helping Powell in lemon investigations in 1909.

45. People whose homes lined the elite drive of the period, Magnolia Avenue.

46. F. Q. Story, President of the Exchange from 1904 to 1920.

47. V. G. Fraser, of Canadian origin, an orange grower, an officer in the Riverside Chamber of Commerce, President of the Riverside Trust Company, and an official in the two local banks. His son, A. W. G. Fraser, became General Manager of the Riverside Orange Company.

48. Dennis' refrigerated railroad car, the first government "reefer," specially designed and ventilated for pre-cooling fruit prior to shipment.

49. Charles Warren Fairbanks, an Indiana railroad lawyer, Vice President under Roosevelt. His son, Fred, was a Redlands rancher.

50. Asa F. Call, Iowa lawyer turned grower in Corona.

51. G. A. Charters, General Eastern Agent of the California Fruit Growers Exchange.

52. Arthur William Foster, native of Ireland, broker, banker, financier, member of the Board of Regents of the University of California, 1900–1930, and Chairman of the Board 1922–1926.

53. An old adobe on the Government Grounds developed in 1864 — a quartermaster's depot, barracks, and stables, with walls twenty-two inches thick.

54. The Potter, one of the famous, leisurely resort hotels of the era, a contrast to the Hayward, a commercial Los Angeles hotel, very successful and busy.

55. Charles C. Teague, manager of the Limoneira Ranch and one of the founders of the lemon industry, whom Powell visited in 1904.

56. Emma Holbrook Clark, married to Gertrude's brother Harold.

57. Louis C. Hill, Supervising Engineer for irrigation projects in the Southwest.

58. Frederick H. Newell, Chief Engineer of the Reclamation Service.

59. The *Riverside Press* for May 10, 1909, mentions the loving cups. The railroad agents who guided the Floridians' trip received solid gold watch fobs.

60. Judge Peter J. Shields of the Sacramento Superior Court.

61. B. B. Pratt, a new member of Powell's team, joining Shamel, Hosford, McKay, and Dennis. Later Chief of the Field Department of the California Fruit Growers Exchange.

62. Allison White Laird, banker, railroad executive, and lumberman in Wisconsin, Washington, and Idaho, where he was general manager of the Potlatch Lumber Co.

63. Powell ignores the existence of Idaho.

64. Of the dozen or more American towns called New Castle or Newcastle, the one Powell refers to is probably New Castle, Delaware.

65. Rep. Francis Wellington Cushman was not succeeded by State Senator Paulhamus, who remained a leader in the State Senate.

66. The Alaska-Yukon-Pacific Exposition of 1909–1910. The United States had a main building and three adjacent structures given to exhibits from Alaska, the Philippines, and Hawaii.

67. On his European trip to study lemon culture in Italy and attend the First International Refrigeration Conference in Paris.

68. The exhibition ventilated railroad car.

69. P. J. Dreher, a Claremont grower.

70. Yucaipa.

71. John Henry Norton, a chemist at the Citrus Experiment Station.

72. At the high school in Riverside Edwin A. Zumbro taught physics, chemistry, German, minerology, and agriculture.

140

Afterword

MY FATHER'S DEATH when I was only fourteen was a lasting trauma. It came as I was leaving boyhood for adolescence and being recognized by him as no longer the child who sat on his lap and lit the match for his Havana. I was ready to take the place of my older brothers who had now become men. My mother told me I was his favorite. There was a special bond between us. I loved the magnetic warmth that made people respond to his leadership and testify to his basic sweetness and kindliness, from Herbert Hoover on down. Then suddenly he was gone.

When in 1938 my oldest brother Clark, already a noted horticulturist in the family tradition, died even younger than his father, I compiled memoirs of him plus his bibliography. My mother asked why I did not do the same for my father. He had been dead only sixteen years, and many were still alive who had worked with him, including Eustace, Stubenrauch, Webber, Shamel, and Francisco. I started to solicit memoirs and listed his publications. I also began to assemble the family papers at UCLA where I was a beginning librarian on the way eventually to head that library.

What emerged was a public figure, not the man I remembered. As my responsibilities increased, other work crowded my father aside. Upon my mother's death in 1957 I inherited the last of the family memorabilia she had preserved through many changes of residence at home and abroad. Included were my father's letters from their Cornell courtship, up to the wartime years in Washington with Hoover when my father drove himself to an early death.

One clutch of letters to her, still in their envelopes, was ribbon-tied and marked "For Lawrence." They were written almost daily from Paris and London in October 1908 when he led the American delegation to the first International Refrigeration Congress, sponsored by the French government. They reported the lively details of his triumphant presentation to the congress and of his fateful meeting

141

with Mary Engle Pennington, a fellow delegate and Quaker from Philadelphia. My mother had told me earlier of that lasting liaison and why she had refused him a divorce. "It was for you boys," she said, "and his career."

Here in those impassioned letters was his response to a newfound Old World and to a new kind of woman-scientist. Here was the warmth I remembered—and also the challenge to write a biography of the whole man. Yet there was so much more I did not know about him or them, and would probably never know. He kept no journal beyond the meager one of that same period; and what other of his correspondence survived was impersonally professional. After outliving him for thirty years, during which she never married, Mary Pennington died in 1952 at eighty, leaving apparently only her professional papers. I was compelled to fill the blanks from memory and imagination. *Portrait of My Father* was a hybrid, both biography and fiction.

Before I wrote it as I was nearing eighty, I transcribed for the first time all of his letters to my mother from before and after 1908. There was only one gap, from his second trip to Europe in 1911 with Frank Chase, son of the beloved pioneer Riverside grower, Ethan Allen Chase. Although my mother's journal for 1911 noted letters and cards from Italy, Sicily, and Spain, none were among her papers, probably lost during her many moves.

I was enthralled by the letters from Southern California, now artfully edited by Professor Lillard. Here was the man to the life, here too was the land of my orange grove boyhood and the Mission Inn I had once claimed as my magic castle. I knew they must be published in memory of him and of the land we loved. Thus would he and his work and a lost land be recalled beyond our time.

Old friendship with Richard Lillard, and respect for his scholarship, led me to ask him to undertake the editing, which he has done to my satisfaction and delight. His portrait of my father is objective and just. Another old friend, Professor Doyce Nunis, flashed the green light when I expressed hope that the Historical Society of Southern California, with which I have had long ties, would include the work among its publications. To them all my deepest thanks.

LAWRENCE CLARK POWELL

University of Arizona
Tucson

PRINTED IN A LIMITED EDITION OF 600 COPIES,
WITH 150 COPIES FOR THE ZAMORANO CLUB AS A KEEPSAKE
FOR THE BIENNIAL JOINT MEETING WITH THE ROXBURGHE CLUB
OF SAN FRANCISCO, OCTOBER 20–21, 1990, IN LOS ANGELES.

SPONSORS

THOMAS F. ANDREWS	DOYCE B. NUNIS, JR.
JOHN CARSON, M.D.	MICHAEL W. NUNN
JAMES F. DICKASON	MARTIN RIDGE
ROBERT L. DOHRMANN	CHARLES RITCHESON
MARVIN FREILICH, M.D.	STUART ROBINSON
RINARD Z. HART, M.D.	JEROME R. SELMER
ROBERT P. HASTINGS	JOHN R. SELMER
ELWOOD W. HOLLAND	HUGH C. TOLFORD
JAMES LORSON	REV. MSGR. FRANCIS J. WEBER
ALDEN H. MILLER, M.D.	